CEDING THE HIGH GROUND

CEDING THE HIGH GROUND
A Nation in Peril

Deceptive promises of peace through compromise have
lured many from their position on the High Moral Ground.
The voices of truth and reason are now being drowned out
on the vast plain of opinion.

Bob Gunderson

XULON PRESS

Xulon Press
2301 Lucien Way #415
Maitland, FL 32751
407.339.4217
www.xulonpress.com

Unless otherwise indicated, Scripture quotations taken from the New American Standard Bible (NASB). Copyright © 1960, 1962, 1963, 1968, 1971, 1972, 1973, 1975, 1977, 1995 by The Lockman Foundation. Used by permission. All rights reserved.

Scripture quotations taken from the King James Version (KJV)–*public domain.*

Printed in the United States of America.

ISBN-13: 978-1-6305-0883-8

Acknowledgments

To my Lord and Savior, Jesus Christ, I owe my all. I have great appreciation for all of His servants who have been instrumental in bringing me along thus far. Foremost on the list is my father, Joel Gunderson, who instilled within me a love for the Scripture. My father's example of the way he approached God's Holy Word established my reverence and carefulness in handling it. He said, "When we depart from a confrontation with the Word of God, it must remain the same as when we came, only we must be different."

There are many others that have been a great inspiration to me through their example of righteous living. I'll be forever indebted to my loving wife who supported me until her dying day. Thanks to my brother Gil, who has always been a rich source of fellowship and sharing in the Word. Thanks to my children who have at times had to endure the inescapable instructions of a father who loves them. And special thanks to Roberta Burns, who helped edit and clean up my manuscript.

Content

Preface

In about 73 AD, legions of Roman soldiers besieged the hilltop fortress of Masada. A small band of Jewish people were able to hold off the Roman army because of their strategic position on high ground. A constructed siege ramp is testimony of the persistence of the Romans to defeat this small group of people. According to the historical account, their strategic position also allowed them to control their own destiny, even in defeat. It was only because of the enormous resources of the Roman army that they were able to conquer this small band of Jewish rebels.

It is common knowledge that those who occupy the high ground have an enormous advantage. One of the things that make the story of Masada so memorable is that this small band of people never left the high ground. Even in defeat they never gave up the high ground, but chose to die there. From their position on the high ground they could assess the strength and size of those who intended to destroy them. They knew where they stood and what they stood for. It is from their stance on the high ground that we can draw inspiration and wisdom for the battles that we face against those who are intent upon destroying us. If we cede the high ground we will lose the strategic position that is so necessary for our survival and victory.

> *"Therefore having been justified by faith, we have peace with God through our Lord Jesus Christ, through whom also we have obtained our introduction by faith into this grace in which we stand; and we exult in hope of the glory of God."* (Ro 5:1-2 NAS)

> *"Be on the alert, stand firm in the faith, act like men, be strong."* (1Co 16:13 NAS)

There is a war going on in this once Christian nation. The very foundation of this nation is under attack as they are attempting to transform who we are as a nation. The Biblical Moral Code, that is the foundation of our governing law and determines who we were as a nation, is under attack. The purpose of the attack is to destroy that foundation, usurping the authority of God and establishing Man's rule as supreme.

This is not a new war, for it has been raging from our beginning and the battles have at times been intense. There have been some critical times in our history as a nation in which a dark cloud hovered over us. In these times it was the truth embedded in our law and culture that helped us to overcome great odds. It seems like each time we recovered from one of these crises that we emerged a little weaker than we had been before. Compromises have been made through the years that have finally brought us to our present crisis that is attempting to complete our transformation to a secular society. For many of the players in this war it is a matter of following an ideological path that they have been convinced will bring about happiness and fulfillment for them. For those who view this war from the high ground, it is clear that this is more than just a battle over ideology and control of our nation. This is a war for men's souls and the consequences are eternal.

Our nation once stood as a sanctuary from tyranny. It was a place where people could freely seek for truth and where the truth could be spoken freely without restriction. Our forefathers believed that if given equal ground, the voice of truth would prevail. Is it any wonder that the first attack on our freedom was to restrict the Word of God? As the enemy gains control of our nation, we are witnessing a purging of the Word of God from our history, classrooms, public squares, and government. How could this happen in the land of the free and the home of the brave? How could the truth fall victim to the lie, if we are free? What has happened?

> *"For our struggle is not against flesh and blood, but against the rulers, against the powers, against the world forces of this darkness, against the spiritual forces of wickedness in the heavenly places."* (Eph 6:12 NAS)

Simply put, those who occupied the high moral ground ceded that ground and were lured to the broad expansive plain of information and opinion. In this expansive plane, the truth was questioned and compromised. Yielding to the multitude, the truth was swept away by the flood. The Law and the Prophets, the two guarding sentinels of our freedoms were removed from our schools, our homes, our government, and finally are being removed from our churches. We forgot who we were up against. We are up against the father of lies and his deceptions. Lured to a lower level it is easy to get focused on people who carry these deceptive lies. Our real battle is against the lies and ideas that are in rebellion to God and His Word. We stood as a nation on the high ground as we acknowledged God. The advantage of the high ground gave us an advantage over all the nations on earth; however, we as a nation have given up that ground and are beginning to suffer the consequences.

There remains a remnant and that remnant is the last and remaining hope for America; however, our numbers are waning and we need to bring people back to their senses. First, we need to understand why we are losing battle after battle; simply put, it is because we are ceding the high moral ground. As soon as we lose the high ground we have lost our advantage. And from the high ground we can have the advantage because we have truth. Truth trumps the lie because it is unchanging. America at one time was bathed in truth. Truth ruled over our science, education, culture, and government.

The voice of the world continues to lure us into compromise and that is why we are losing battles. A truth compromised is not the truth. Time has shown that truth compromised succumbs to the bold lie. We must reverse the present trend or we will end up as Israel did, with a small band occupying the high ground. There on that high moral ground they stood firm. Likewise, we must stand firm as a testimony of righteousness as the armies of political correctness seek to snuff out the voice of truth in America.

Follow me as I attempt to define that High Moral Ground and encourage people to head to that ground. Standing on this ground, we insure our personal safety and position ourselves to reveal and expose the enemy of our souls. If we stand our ground, we will be successful. The degree of that success will depend upon how many we can convince to join us. Can our nation be saved? I know it can be because there is a Savior who is willing. Will our nation be saved? If those who have left the high moral ground will simply return to their position of safety, then this nation will be confronted with truth. If our Nation will once again acknowledge God and repent, then our nation will be saved.

Many people and churches have lost their advantage to influence the culture around them. The lies of the enemy have lured them to a lower level to fight the battle for truth on the world's level. Battered with arguments on the world's level has actually caused Christians to be ashamed of righteousness. We are chided and accused of looking down on people. Of course we look down on them, because we have the advantage of the high ground, but we do not look down on them as they would imagine we do. If we did, we would not be on the high moral ground. From our vantage, we see souls in bondage and our desire is to bring them all up to a higher plain, a place of peace and safety. If we cede the high ground, we begin to look just like them and we have lost our advantage to bring a healing influence to the world around us.

How can we win if we cede the high ground and lose our advantage?

Introduction

Living in the Real World

We live in a time of tremendous advances in technology. It is easy to be so intoxicated with the momentum of advances in technology that we sometimes forget that there are fundamental principles that never change. In fact, it is these principles that make it possible for all these advances. It does not matter what field we examine, understanding the fundamental principles involved gives us an advantage.

Hand in hand with the advances in technology has been the accumulation of knowledge. It is this accumulation of knowledge that has given rise to technology that allows us to preserve that knowledge, and increasingly allows us better and faster access to that knowledge. You would think that sooner or later this incredible momentum would eventually peak. At present it has not appeared to be slowing down anytime soon. This is a blessing and a curse at the same time.

We have been blessed with an abundance of technological gadgets. Some of them are very useful, some intriguing and interesting, and some just entertaining. We are now able to view and virtually experience the world around us without leaving our living room. We have an incredible amount of knowledge accessible at the tip of our fingers. We can travel to most parts of the earth within hours or at least days. Luxury and the most exotic products in the world are limited only by the size of your bank account.

Has all of this been too much too soon? There have been some serious drawbacks from this influx of technology. For one thing, the younger generations seem to be developing, in large part, into a bunch of spoiled brats. They seem to lack appreciation for everything that has just been handed to them with little or no effort on their part. Cultural changes are taking place at seemingly lightning speed. We are flooded with an endless stream of news events. To take it all in, important information is often reduced to video clips and sound bites.

Even though we have a vast amounts of knowledge at our fingertips, it is mixed with just as much or more information that is not true. Then there are all the various opinions blended with the facts. Many of these opinions are based upon ideology rather than an assessment of the facts.

The same technology that allows us to explore the utmost regions of the world around us also makes it possible to virtually create illusions out of our utmost fantasy. Through technology the extreme imaginations of the mind can appear as reality before our eyes. In many different ways, technology is separating people from the physical realities of our world.

All these things and more allow those who gain control of the various medias to manipulate our very perception of reality. The questions then arise; are our conclusions based upon what we know, or on what we think we know? There has been a dramatic change in the direction of our thinking in the last 50 years. Is this a result of increased knowledge, or have we become victims of an alternate reality that only exists in our imagination?

This will seem like a strange introduction to the topic I am about to discuss; however, a brief glance at the mental attitudes that prevail in our country today may be a helpful reminder before beginning any of the dozen different discussions I would like to have with the people of these United States. With the introduction of the idea that all truth is relative, our nation is rapidly losing its ability to come to rational conclusions. What is ironic is that every advance in science or technology is based upon the fact that truth is constant and unchanging. It is truly mind boggling that while we live in this age of amazing scientific discovery and technological advances, the idea that truth is relative persists and advances.

I could write a book documenting the numerous ways that people are finding to live in an alternate reality of their own imagination; however, my focus here is going to be toward the dwindling number of people who have had a conservative bent. People who have recognized that the God of the Bible is that one constant that makes the world we live in logical and the voice of nature coherent. This is the group of people who, by virtue of embracing truth, hold the moral high ground. It is important that we do not cede that high moral ground as many are doing. It is only from this position that we can instill rationality into a world that is in the process of self-destructing.

**"For false Christs and false prophets will arise
and will show great signs and wonders, so
as to mislead, if possible, even the elect."**
(Mt 24:24 NAS)

Jesus warned us so that we would not be swayed by illusions and delusions. Never before in all of history has it been so easy to make an illusion appear to be real. It is only our faith in God and His Word that will keep us sane. It is our faith in God's Word that will enable us to distinguish between that which is real and that which is deception. Considering things in the context of God's Word is of utmost importance. Context makes all the difference. A man standing on a manure pile may look like he is on high ground in Kansas, but in the context of the Colorado Rockies his true height is exposed. Dig a little deeper into what is holding him up and you will see it is not rock-solid either. Only truth will survive in the context of God's Word.

CHAPTER 1
Sound Doctrine — Eternal Truth

"I charge [thee] therefore before God, and the Lord Jesus Christ, who shall judge the quick and the dead at his appearing and his kingdom; Preach the word; be instant in season, out of season; reprove, rebuke, exhort with all longsuffering and doctrine. For the time will come when they will not endure sound doctrine; but after their own lusts shall they heap to themselves teachers, having itching ears; And they shall turn away [their] ears from the truth, and shall be turned unto fables." (2Ti 4:1-4 AV)

We live in a time when people will not endure sound doctrine. It is often ignored, and in many instances, despised. I am not talking here about those who blatantly reject Christ and his teachings, but those who claim to be "Christian". Jesus' prayer for His people is that we would be sanctified (separated) by truth. He defined that truth saying, "Thy Word is Truth". What should then be the distinguishing mark of a Christian is that they are living in a manner that reflects the truth as revealed in God's Word.

Right and Wrong

In a word, what I am writing about is "morality", "right and wrong", and "good and evil". How do we determine what is good and what is evil? Of course, our determination is based in large part by our "world view". Our world view will determine whether we base morality upon the revelation in the Bible, or another ideology created by philosophical thinkers, or we possibly look toward science to answer these questions?

For the Christian the answer is clear. The Bible is the revelation from God, the creator of all things, who has defined right and wrong behavior. If we then apply science by considering the facts involved, and analyzing the ramification of this revealed morality, then I believe we have added confirmation. If we choose to look at this morality from a philosophical perspective, then we would also find reasonable justification for Biblical morality, for it is able to fulfill the goals of peace and contentment for not only individuals, but society as a whole.

Origin of the Moral Code

Historically, this moral code of behavior existed from the very beginning. Man was created good, so he just naturally did good. It was his disobedience in eating the fruit of the tree of the knowledge of good and evil, that opened the door for bad behavior. Immediately upon sinning, Adam and Eve knew they had sinned. They had violated their very nature.

Often, historians point back to the Law of Moses, which was handed to him on Mount Sinai. This is the source of the written moral code that we have today, but any serious analysis reveals that the code has existed from the very beginning. The Apostle Paul's writings say that no one is without excuse, for attributes of a holy God are revealed to us in nature. He goes on to say that every man was also given a conscience, knowing right from wrong. The necessity for spelling out the commandment came because of man's rebellion. The code of morality, from heaven, is not just an arbitrary set of rules, but is a reflection of the character of the Creator Himself. Everything in the universe was created orderly and in harmony with everything else. It was sin that disrupted that order and harmony.

Evolution–A Way of Thinking

We live at a time when life is viewed through an evolutionary perspective. It was during the mid-1800's that biological evolution was clearly articulated and began its rise to popularity. We have made tremendous advances in science since then. Science has unlocked many of the secrets of the world in which we live, allowing us to create technological marvels, and to have insight into the vast universe that surrounds us. In spite of the fact that our advances are based upon understanding of the laws that govern the universe, the myth of evolution continues to dominate modern thought. It doesn't seem to faze the proponents of this myth that it violates all of the laws that govern the universe. Observational science reveals a world and universe that is in a state of decay, devolving rather than evolving.

I mention this because the evolutionary mindset has permeated every field of thought. As with any false concept, false proof is propagated by illusion. A clear example of this is seen in the testimony given in the famous Scopes trial. When presenting an argument for the evolution of simple organisms to complex organisms, the following example was used: We see this process happening every day as a person evolves from a single cell to a complex human being.

In light of our present knowledge of genetics, this argument seems absolutely ridiculous. We now know that a single cell, after fertilization, contains all of the information of the mature individual. That simple fertilized egg not only has all of the complex information about every detail of the individual that is yet unformed, but also contains the information to make it happen. We also know that when we consider simpler life forms, there is no such thing as a simple life form. Then, of course, there is the challenge of finding a mechanism to add information to an organism to make it into something else.

Present knowledge also sheds light on the illusion of evolution through survival of the fittest. The illusion is shattered when we become aware that selective breeding, whether natural or man-directed, is actually a loss of genetic information. The information can only be regained by breeding back the (deselected) traits.

I offer these examples because the evolutionary mindset has seemly permeated every other field of study. Evolutionary theory was devised to explain biology, but has since been applied to the inorganic also, as in the field of astronomy. The vast universe was proposed as coming from nothing, at best a result from a giant explosion. It doesn't seem to matter that evolving complexity and organization, seem to defy all of the laws of physics as we know them. The theory prevails in spite of evidence, not because of it.

Evolutionary thinking is often applied in many different fields of study, whether it be religion, philosophy or history. In some ways, it may be a natural way for us as humans to think about things. We enter the world in ignorance and accumulate knowledge over time. Our understanding evolves over time as we learn and experience the world around us. Our means of passing on what we have learned to the next generation has also evolved over time. Evolving technology has exploded in our day and flooded us with information. We marvel at modern inventions like the automobile, or the computer, and can trace their historical evolution.

I want to bring your attention to the difference between theoretical evolution and actual evolution. Theoretical evolution exists only in the imagination. Actual evolution is the result of discovery and application. Our knowledge base, and the things that we create, have been able to evolve simply because truth, and the laws that govern the universe, are constant and not evolving. The other important factor to consider about actual evolution is that the abilities we have been created with are what allow us to discover and apply knowledge. If you take these two factors out of the equation, how long would the evolution of the automobile and the computer taken? They simply would not have evolved. They not only could not have created themselves, there was no reason or purpose for them to exist.

Evolutionary theory has no basis in science. In fact, it stands in contradiction to the laws we are beginning to understand through our discovery process. Nevertheless, it has become very popular in our present day cultures of the world, as men seek to distance themselves from their Creator. The application of this erroneous theory to morals, has allowed many to be deceived into believing the illusion that they hold the high moral ground. It is truth that can shatter their destructive illusion, and that is what is most needed in our world today.

Back to the Source

If we want to know and understand the moral code, we must go back to where it exists in its purest form. The concepts of right and wrong have been toyed with and manipulated, since the fall of man in the Garden of Eden. Many have been deceived into thinking that the understanding of right and wrong has been a process of trial and error, in which we are now approaching the pinnacle of morality. History reveals just the opposite; rather, people have a tendency to stray from the moral standard. Mankind's drift from that standard has always resulted in chaos and destruction. It has only been because of the repentant souls, who have joined together to re-establish that moral standard, that we have at times been able, to a degree, to lift man back to a semblance of the dignity for which he was designed for.

In C. S. Lewis's "Mere Christianity," he makes a case for the Moral Law, or the Law of Right and Wrong. He shows how it exists in every time and place. His conclusion is that when we consider the reality of this law, it is obvious that it comes from outside of ourselves. Yet it is as real as our behavior, as real as gravity. When we deny that this law exists, we have the same results as when we deny that gravity exists. There are consequences; peace and safety will never exist unless groups of people agree to follow the moral law.

I touch on C. S. Lewis's masterful explanation of the Moral Law because he shows clearly that the Law did not originate with us. This is God's Law, and that is why we are often uncomfortable talking about it. It is easier for us to recognize this Law than it is to follow it. When we come close to following it, we are recognized as decent civilized persons. If morality had originated with man and evolved over time, wouldn't we be able to look back and see how far we had come? The horseless carriage has evolved over the last 100 years, but morality, or decent behavior, is the same as it was in the Garden of Eden.

God's Law – Man's Law

"For since the creation of the world His invisible attributes, His eternal power and divine nature, have been clearly seen, being understood through what has been made, so that they are without excuse." (Ro 1:20 NAS95)

The laws that govern the universe, both physical and spiritual, are revelations of God's attributes, His eternal power, and His divine nature. Those laws concerning our behavior define morality or goodness for us. They are a reflection of the very nature of God Himself. In 1 John 1:8 the nature of God is defined in a word, "God is Love". All of Scripture is expounding upon the Law of Love, bringing us revelation and insight into that Law.

Without this Law there is chaos. Adherence to this Law brings peace and safety.

Then there are the laws that govern the societies on earth. This is mankind's law. This law is ever-changing, evolving and devolving. The success of man's law to bring about a peaceful society is closely linked to its adherence to the principles of God's Law. More importantly, is the degree in which the societal members embrace the spirit of that law.

You Can't Legislate Morality?

It seems like in every election cycle there is someone who makes the statement that you cannot legislate morality. In reality, **Law is the legislation of morality**. What allows people to think that morality cannot be legislated is the fact that laws do not make people moral. A person is moral because they adhere to the Law. If there is no respect for the law and no one who can enforce it, then the effect on society is minimal and it remains only as a reminder in a lawless society.

The effect of not upholding righteous law has dire consequences. Someone pays for the breaking of the law. The affected person or persons, we call the victims. The effects of unlawful actions are usually far-reaching because no man is an island. The lawbreaker himself is affected in ways he would not choose to admit, even when he eludes exposure. There is no such thing as a victimless crime. When God's laws are ignored, it does not nullify the consequences. When a society fails to incorporate the laws of God in their legal system, it creates a situation where the people are ignorant of why they are suffering.

Freeing people of the knowledge of the law does not free them from the consequences of breaking the law.

It is interesting that those who adamantly object to having God's law as a part of the legal system, still seem to want their concept of right and wrong to be legislated. The irony is that in an effort to avoid the Ten Commandments, lawmakers have created a system of hundreds of thousands of laws. All of those laws together are not as effective as the implementation of the Ten Commandments would be. It is the goals and focus of those who create the laws that determine the outcome.

The goal of God's law is righteousness. The fruit of righteousness includes peace and safety. The goals of man's laws are control and manipulation for power and money. The appetite of the unrighteous is never satisfied, for it is fueled by envy and greed. The fruit of man's system is confusion and unrest. Truth, freedom and security are the victims. Man's quest for happiness often leads to unrighteousness. A quest for righteousness leads to peace, contentment and happiness.

Law, Laws, and Legalism

The word, law, is often used in a generic sense to include ordinances, statutes, commands, precepts and judgments. There is a deeper meaning of law. Science has defined some of those laws which enable us to understand the universe in which we live. These are the laws that define the existence of everything we know. The existence of everything depends upon the fact that these laws never change. The order and design of everything in the universe must fit within these parameters to remain viable.

A lot of what we call law is merely an attempt to protect us from violating the actual, absolute laws. As an example, consider the law that requires us to stop at a stop light. The real laws we are trying to protect people from have to do with the fact that two cars cannot occupy the same space at the same time, without being seriously disorganized.

When people strictly focus on those ordinances and statutes that are there to protect us from violating the actual laws, then they become legalistic. As time goes on, people sometimes forget what the legal system is supposed to be all about. It is possible to be so engrossed in the legal system that people actually become ignorant of the real laws. That is what I call legalism. You can be operating fully within the legal system as you drive your car, but if you do not yield to someone who violates a stop signal, then you may end up dead right. The physical law trumps the paper laws.

Spiritual Law, Laws, and Legalism

We have to start with the physical to help us understand the spiritual. It is easier for us to understand the physical because this is what we can see and feel. The spiritual is just as real. We are body, soul and spirit. So much in the universe simply defies explanation without the acknowledgment of the spiritual. Without the Spirit of God, nothing would exist. We who were created in the image and likeness of God, exist as humans because God breathed the breath of life into us. Science that denies the reality of the spiritual, cannot explain our emotional and spiritual awareness that promotes morality. As earlier stated, we are all born with a fundamental understanding that there is such a thing as right and wrong.

Just as there are physical laws around which everything is organized and designed, it is the same in the spiritual. There are spiritual laws that must be adhered to. Much of the Scripture is for the purpose of protecting us from violating those spiritual laws, which when violated result in death.

> *""I gave them My statutes and informed them of My ordinances, by which, if a man observes them, he will live."* (Eze 20:11 NAS95)

Those of us that are familiar with the Scripture, are aware that all have sinned and violated the laws of God. Even from the beginning, God, in His mercy, intended to provide a way of salvation and freedom from the law of sin and death. We know that salvation came through the sacrificial death of Jesus Christ, on the Cross, and His resurrection to life. That salvation is received today by the same pattern that was laid down in the Old Testament. You can see from these two quotes that that the call for repentance was the same in the Old Testament as in the New Testament.

> *"But if the wicked man turns from all his sins which he has committed and observes all My statutes and practices justice and righteousness, he shall surely live; he shall not die."* (Eze 18:21 NAS95)

11

> *"But the things which God announced beforehand by the mouth of all the prophets, that His Christ would suffer, He has thus fulfilled. "Therefore repent and return, so that your sins may be wiped away, in order that times of refreshing may come from the presence of the Lord; and that He may send Jesus, the Christ appointed for you,"* (Ac 3:18-20 NAS95)

Sin, in its many forms, is a violation of the spiritual law. Jesus gave us the essence of that law when He answered the question about the great commandment.

> *"And He said to him, "'YOU SHALL LOVE THE LORD YOUR GOD WITH ALL YOUR HEART, AND WITH ALL YOUR SOUL, AND WITH ALL YOUR MIND.' "This is the great and foremost commandment. "The second is like it, 'YOU SHALL LOVE YOUR NEIGHBOR AS YOURSELF.' "On these two commandments depend the whole Law and the Prophets."* (Mt 22:37-40 NAS95)

God is love, and for His creation to violate that fundamental law that governs the universe, has as a consequence, death. The Law and the Prophets reveal to us how we have and oftentimes violated the Law of Love, or as James puts it, "The Royal Law". The Ten Commandments give us a brief outline. Much of the rest of the Scripture goes into greater detail.

As with the physical laws, people can get so focused on the ordinances and statutes that they seem to forget these things are mere tools to protect us from the consequences of breaking the actual law. If our focus is strictly on the ordinances and statutes, we come across to those around us as being legalistic. Although legalism is fundamentally no different in spiritual law than it is in physical law, it is much more obvious in the area of spiritual law. This is simply because, as fallen creatures, we are more in tune with the physical realm than we are with the spiritual realm.

Consequently, in our culture of declining moral values, being tagged as legalistic has become a point of shame and humiliation, even in Christian circles. The effect has been that many have abandoned any talk about those statutes and ordinances, that at one time were effective for teaching people about the Law of God.

True knowledge of the law of God brings an understanding of the importance of the ordinances and statutes, that form a safety net for us. Following those ordinances and statutes helps keep us from violating God's Law, and helps us teach others of His Law. The true follower of God's Law unashamedly follows, and teaches others to follow the ordinances, statutes and commands found in God's Word. A true follower of Christ may appear legalistic, but what sets them apart is their motivation of love for God and man.

Spiritual legalism will no more save you than physical legalism, although there are temporary benefits, simply because they are good practices to do. Eventually, we will face some real tests that confirm our adherence to the real law. It is in those supposed gray areas that we come to find out how well we really understand the Law of God. Just like the city boy who drives his car out into the country; when the lines end and the traffic signals disappear, will he drive his car into a tree or off of a cliff? Legalism only provides a buffer so far, and no farther.

The Moral High Ground

"Jesus Christ is the same yesterday and today and forever." (Heb 13:8 NAS95)

I have been trying to build a case for the moral high ground. I think everyone would agree that there is such a thing as right and wrong, but not everyone would agree that there is a standard right and wrong. I contend that there is a single point of authority from which morality stems. That point of authority is God, the creator of all things. The Scripture also teaches us that God never changes, but always remains the same. Because God is eternal and unchanging, morality is also constant and unchanging. The physical world testifies of God's unchanging nature. Science is based upon His unchanging laws. That is why when we do an experiment in a controlled environment, we can predict the outcome with perfect accuracy.

Acknowledging God as the governing authority establishes the standard moral high ground. There can be no doubt as to what is right and wrong when God, Himself, declares it to be so. To establish a different moral code requires us to usurp the authority of the Creator. The challenge for the high ground has occurred time after time throughout history. The challenges come on many levels and always with the same results. All challenges fall far short, but for some reason they continue. The fact still remains as stated in the Scripture:

> *"Every good gift and every perfect gift is from above, and cometh down from the Father of lights, with whom is no variableness, neither shadow of turning."* (Jas 1:17 AV)

Free Will

Is the gift of choice a blessing, or a curse? Yes, it is a blessing and a curse. We are blessed when we make the right choice, and we are cursed when we make the wrong choice. Herein is the distinction between the physical realm and the spiritual realm. The physical choices often have immediate results. Everything is required to submit to the laws of physics that govern the universe. In the spiritual realm, our rebellious choices result in consequences that are not always detected immediately; however, be sure that your sin will find you out. Those consequences are usually farther reaching than the violation of the physical laws. Likewise, spiritual death is much more serious than that of physical death.

Life would be so much less complicated, if there was no choice. What if we could choose whether or not we had choice? What would we choose? Would we wish to be happy little robots? Maybe we would have to be happy. This philosophical bantering will get us no place; however, I think that because we were created in the image and likeness of God, we would not be happy if we did not have choice.

Not only did God gift us with choice, but when that choice was linked to right and wrong, He clearly articulated the consequences of a wrong choice. In spite of God's warnings, man chose to rebel. Man's rebellion affected even the physical world in which we live. All of us have to live with the consequences of sin every day. Of course, the final consequence is death, but God, in His mercy, has provided a way of escape through our Savior Jesus Christ.

Because of God's provision through Christ, He has restored to us the ability of choice in the most important area. We can choose life through faith in Christ Jesus. Our final redemption comes at the return of our Lord and Savior. Until then, we continue to live in this world that has been affected by sin, and inhabited by sinners.

Man sometimes questions why God would allow this world to continue with all of its wickedness and sin. For me, the answer to that question comes when I see a sinner repenting before God and experiencing the transformation of a new life in Christ. God continues to seek and to save those who are lost.

There are two scenarios being lived out in our world every day that testify of the righteousness of God. One is that when men refuse to live by the laws that govern the universe, people suffer. There is such a direct correlation between these two facts that you would wonder why people continue to sin. If you are wondering why men continue down this destructive path, in spite of the historical record, it is usually because of pride. Instead of accepting responsibility for their actions, people tend to blame God; or they find some other scapegoat or victims they can take advantage of. The bottom line is that a lot of our problems are the direct result of sin.

The second scenario is when a person, or group of people, decide to strictly adhere to God's law, they reap many blessings. This is true on a personal level, to which I can testify. On a larger scale, it can be even more dramatic. The history of Israel gives us a long running example of what happens when a nation chooses right, and when they choose wrong. Likewise, the United States can track its history and see the effect of following God's law or ignoring it. We have paid a great price as a nation for the early days of slavery. On the flip side, we have been blessed like no other people on earth, when we as a nation acknowledged God and promoted righteousness.

> *"I call heaven and earth to witness against you today, that I have set before you life and death, the blessing and the curse. So choose life in order that you may live, you and your descendants,"* (De 30:19 NAS95)

CHAPTER 2
The High Moral Ground

The Attack

It is recorded that when the world was young, there arose in the garden that God had planted, a serpent, with a cunning agenda. His aim was to pervert God's creation and destroy God's plan for man. His relentless attack has continued to this day.

To his disappointment, there has always been a man willing to stand firmly, unapologetic, on the moral high ground. There was Abel, Seth, Enoch, and then Noah, who alone stood in his generation. Then there was Shem, Abraham, Isaac, and Jacob. Even to this day there are those men who occupy the moral high ground because they have put their trust in the author and finisher of our faith. All of these are an inspiration for us to put our faith in God. With His enablement, we can rise to the high ground and stand firm on that moral high ground.

It is important that we understand the nature of the attack, for the elements of the attack have not changed. The lie was introduced subtly, questioning the motivation of God. The serpent presented his proposal as representing the moral high ground. The serpent proposed that God does not want you to rise to His level, so He has imposed rules to keep you down in your place.

The idea was to plant doubt in Eve's mind about the love of God. Satan's strategy was to narrow Eve's view to the one thing that was forbidden. "Has God not said that you shall not eat of every tree in the garden?" Eve's answer was: "We can eat of every tree in the garden except the tree in the middle of the garden". Eve even gave the reason why they must not eat of that particular tree. "We can't eat of that tree because God forbade us to eat of it. He forbade us because; if we ate from it we would die". Satan replied, "You will not surely die, for God knows that when you eat of it your eyes will be opened and you will be as gods knowing good and evil."

Notice the subtly in which Satan mixes fact with fantasy. The result is that Eve's focus is diverted from the generous blessings of a loving God to the one thing that has been forbidden. As Eve considers the forbidden fruit as a source of food and wisdom, her faith in God falters and she rebels. The promised result comes in a most unexpected way. Her eyes are opened and she knows sin.

Adam likewise succumbs to the voice of his wife, the voice of experience, and sins against God by partaking of the forbidden fruit. Now they know what God knows about the effect that fruit would have on them. Obviously it was not as satisfying as they had been deceived into believing. Their innocence had been violated. They experienced a profound self-awareness, that they were naked. They experienced fear for the first time, as God approached them. Their eyes were indeed opened in a way that was not good. They had brought a curse on themselves and on all of creation. They were going to die and a part of them had already died. They were no longer innocent.

The high ground of morality or righteousness is founded on love. God is the God of Love. God is love. God's purpose for mankind has always been in man's best interest and God in his wisdom knows what is best for us. When Eve retreated from that moral high ground of trust in the God of love, she lost that high ground and brought Adam down with her.

The High Ground

Few subjects are more important than those dealing with and determining right and wrong, for the accepted morality of a society is foundational to its very existence. It is important in any serious discussion that people understand the basic terms being used. When I am referring to the moral high ground, I am speaking of those concepts that are most easily defended because they present undisputable truth. I realize that there are people that will argue that 2+2 does not equal 4, but there are some arguments that do not even merit a reply.

It is obvious that we are in a battle of world views. Although many times in history men have ended up on a physical battlefield, the battle always starts with conflicting ideas and concepts. Because we are moral beings, we tend to try to defend our position, first in our own mind, and then with those we hope to align with us. I have already presented some general concepts of what is moral. As we continue this discussion, I will get a little more specific in my defense of right and wrong as revealed to us in Scripture.

My reference to the "high ground" is taken from those physical battles that have been waged throughout history. Modern warfare with airplanes and missiles is beginning to blur this concept of occupying the high ground, but I am sure we have not totally lost this concept that was so important for so long. The concept is still true in modern warfare, but just not as easily captured in clear imagery.

There is tremendous advantage of occupying the high ground. We can start with the view you have from this perspective. From this viewpoint you have a better understanding and an overall view of the entire situation. You might say that you are on top of it. You have the advantage of not being taken by surprise because you can see everything coming at you. From your high perch you have a circumspect view. You are not limited by a narrow perspective. Your position is easily defended. It does not matter from which angle you are attacked. You are on top of it and can see it coming. From this position you can call the shots. You can either wait for the enemy to approach you, or you can go on the offensive. When the actual fighting begins you have the advantage of fighting downhill. The enemy has an uphill battle.

If you want to enhance the image I am trying to create, then look to that fortress in the Judean desert, Masada. Here a small group of Jews were able to hold off the might of the Roman military machine. This small group of people set the standard for uncompromising defense of what was important to them. Even in defeat no one was able to violate their resolve to not surrender. They never left the high ground. This was their land and their heritage, and they stuck to it.

Acquiring the High Ground

How do we acquire the status of occupying the moral high ground? I have in a sense already answered this question. It is not a matter of superior intellect, acquired knowledge, or vast experience. It is merely accepting the standard that has been handed down to us from God Himself. It is simply putting our trust in God. I like the words of the song writer penned in that old hymn, "Higher Ground".

Lord, lift me up and let me stand
By faith on Heaven's table land,
A higher plane than I have found;
Lord, plant my feet on higher ground.

We arrive on this higher ground by simply having faith in God and trusting His Word. I am not talking about a blind faith that is better described as wishful thinking. I am talking about trust in the Word of God that has proven to be true over and over throughout the course of time.

It does not matter if we have arrived here tentatively or with great resolve, the high ground is the high ground. How we came to this position often determines how solidly we arrive here. What is important is, that once we have arrived, that we plant our feet here. My purpose in writing is to help establish people's confidence in this plane, even if they have arrived tentatively. I also want to make sure that none of us take for granted our status and allow ourselves to get too close to the edge whereby we start slipping down that slippery slope toward destruction.

I want to keep reminding you that the foundation of true morality is love. This is based upon the very character of God and that is why morality is eternal rather than evolutionary. We must keep this in mind as we study the different facets of morality.

War of the World Views

Since the first attack on morality (the law of God) the war of world views has persisted. Often the battles have been hard fought as the forces of hell attempt to thwart the plan of God. If it were not for the grace and mercy of God, our world would have gone the way of the world of Noah's day and destroyed itself; however, God has intervened. Through revivals and an occasional reboot, He has kept hope of righteousness alive all of these years.

The attack of Satan in the Garden of Eden started the conflict that is with us to this day. Through the deceptive lie, Satan introduced the accusation that God's moral law was intended to restrict Man and limit his potential. Of course the opposite was true, for the Law of God is the Law of Love. Its intent is to protect and preserve mankind in an atmosphere of fellowship with God and all of creation.

If we can grasp the nature of the conflict, then we will understand why both sides battle so differently. Satan's attack is focused on the foundation of the Law, which is love. His aim is to convince people that God's law is not based upon love. If the foundation is undermined, then morality will begin to collapse. Satan is unrestricted by truth or love as he mocks and ridicules people or makes promises that remain unfulfilled. On the other hand, those who live by God's law are bound by love.

The battle is for our preservation and to win those who are blinded by the lies of Satan. Armed with the truth, we seek to convince those in darkness to come to the light, to trust God and choose life. Motivated by love, we testify of the grace of God and warn of the judgment to come.

CHAPTER 3
IMPORTANT HISTORICAL NOTES

Division by Nations

S oon after the flood the peoples of the world, in rebellion against God, determined to unite in an effort to build a city and a tower, to become mighty as god upon the earth. God intervened by confusing their language. From here the nations of the earth were established, providing a barrier for Satan's ambitious plan to unite mankind in rebellion to God's rule. History shows us the persistence of Satan to inspire men to fulfill his goal of a one world government. Up until now he has failed with every attempt, yet he persists. Globalism is again gaining momentum in our day. The underlying philosophy that is often obscured is the replacement of the rule of God by a world government. Those with insight understand that it is Satan that is behind this movement and his desire is to exercise dominion over the pinnacle of God's creation, Man.

There are two despised enemies of Satan's plan, the Hebrew people and the Church. Even after the Jewish rejection of Christ as Messiah, God still has a plan for the Children of Abraham. As long as they can be identified as a people they stand as a witness of the righteousness of God. They have been attacked from without and within, yet a remnant still remains.

The Church likewise has suffered from attacks from without and within. The most vicious attacks have been from within. Yet there remains and continues to rise up a people faithful to the righteousness of God, an uncompromising people who have put their trust and confidence in their Lord Jesus Christ.

A Nation Set Apart

"Now the LORD said to Abram, "Go forth from your country, And from your relatives And from your father's house, To the land which I will show you; And I will make you a great nation, And I will bless you, And make your name great; And so you shall be a blessing; And I will bless those who bless you, And the one who curses you I will curse. And in you all the families of the earth will be blessed." (Ge 12:1-3 NAS95)

History only records two nations that have been birthed on the foundational Law of God, nations whose king was to be the Lord himself. Of these two, Israel is the only one created in purity of source and purpose. It was on God's initiative that Abram was chosen, separated, and commissioned. Abram accepted God's call and stepped forward in faith and obedience, following the direction and guidance from God.

From the outset until our present day God has used this nation to reveal to the world the righteousness of God, the sinfulness of man, and God's plan for redemption. God has taken and preserved this small nation and a small piece of ground as a witness and reminder to all the earth of the eternal truths. This tiny

26

nation preserved outside of their homeland for two thousand years, now is becoming established on their God-designated land. Their very existence continues to confound the World. Their existence defies all explanations, except one, God. King Frederick the Great once asked his physician Zimmermann of Brugg-in-Aargau, "Zimmermann, can you name me a single proof of the existence of God?" The physician replied, "Your majesty, the Jews."

From Abram, to Moses, to David and Solomon, to the destruction of Jerusalem, to the rebuilding of Jerusalem, to the rejection of the Messiah, to destruction and dispersal, to the holocaust, to present-day Israel, God has used Israel for his purpose. Israel has been God's source of revelation to the whole world. God's intention is blessing. Man's rejection brings a curse. Israel has been an example of righteousness and blessing, sin and judgment, and a source of blessing and a source of judgment. Through Israel God has given us the Law and the Prophets, a revelation of righteousness and judgment. Most importantly God has used Israel to reveal His love and mercy. God has laid out his plan for forgiveness, redemption, restoration, and eternal life through His Son Jesus, the Christ.

Those nations that have been a blessing to Israel have been blessed. Those nations who have cursed Israel have been cursed. To this present day the ramifications of actions for or against Israel have had their consequences. When Israel prospers the whole world is afforded opportunity to share in those blessings. When they are oppressed the whole world suffers.

Diaspora and the Church

"Therefore I say to you, the kingdom of God will be taken away from you and given to a people, producing the fruit of it." (Mt 21:43 NAS95)

Israel had been entrusted with the Word of God. But when the Word appeared to them in human form, a form easily understood, they rejected Him. Make no mistake, Jesus was not saying He was taking the kingdom away from the Jews and giving it to the Gentiles, because He gave the kingdom to a group of Jews. Jesus was addressing the chief priests and Pharisees and their leadership of the Nation of Israel. The kingdom of God on earth was now directed through the disciples since God established the Church on the day of Pentecost. Under God's direction the Church broadened its appeal to the Gentiles also. As the Apostle Paul later stated, God broke down the barrier of separation and of the two made one; one shepherd, one flock. Under the leadership of the Apostles, God's kingdom on earth multiplied producing the fruit of that kingdom.

The significance of Jesus' life, ministry, death, and resurrection, is so profound and important that all of man's existence is now measured from the time of His birth. God's plan for the redemption of mankind was fulfilled in Jesus Christ. The Jewish nation that had been so instrumental in bringing this to pass was sent into the Diaspora (the scattering abroad of the Jews from their homeland). The birth of the Church on the day of Pentecost began an outreach of evangelism that continues to this day.

With the Diaspora, the nation of Israel faded to the background for about two thousand years only to reappear in our present generation. The Church had phenomenal expansion during the first couple of generations following Christ's resurrection. Persecution and opposition seemed to mark its very existence, and at times accelerated its spread and strengthened its members.

The expanding Church faced many perils. Foremost of these perils came when it was embraced by kings and rulers. Compromise and subtlety have often been marks of the attacks from Satan. Once the exclusive Lordship of Christ in the Church was compromised it became a tool in the hands of kings to rule their people. In spite of this perversion of the mission of the Church, the message of the gospel survived, even if at times it had to go underground. God's Word does not return to Him void. There remained a remnant of the faithful, and the mission of the Church continued at various paces and places throughout history.

We can look at this period of time from the first century Christianity until the Reformation from several perspectives. Indeed, volumes have been written of the interaction of Christianity and society through this time period. At times it seemed to restrain rulers and at times it seemed to enable them in their quests to conquer and dominate the world around them. My point in mentioning this time is not to delve into the multifaceted interactions of the Church at different places at different times. I simply wish to point out that the world was a different place because the Church was here. The Church was a reminder to the world of that which does not change. A reminder that there was a law that was higher than the rule of kings on earth.

The Church's institutions at times became corrupted, aligning themselves with evil men. But through it all God's Word was preserved. At times the light seem to flicker, but never was entirely extinguished. There were always enemies that seemed intent on destroying God's Word. But God's Word remained unchanging, faithful, and true. It continued, often behind the scenes, to uphold and inspire faith and hope.

Reformation

Even in the darkest times there were always those voices, inspired by God, calling men to repentance. And there were those in every period of history that heeded that call and in their generation stood as testimonies of God's mercy and grace. As the Church rose to political heights it also descended to spiritual depths. Organizations that claimed to be the Church of God became the persecutors and tormentors of the children of God.

It was on the testimonies and mangled bodies of these witnesses that God was able to reignite the gospel to a sick and dying world. It was the powerful, never changing, Word of God that ignited the reformation of a people who carried God's name but knew Him not. With the invention of the printing press in the 15th century, the Word was able to bypass those who would pervert it and make it into the hands and hearts of the people. It took the world by storm and created divisions and conflicts. Efforts to quell these movements were unsuccessful as they began springing up all over.

It is only looking back on these events that we can see how the timing of these events would be so significant in opening the door of freedom for mankind and the spreading of the gospel. As the truth of the Word of God was being revived a new land was being opened up to plant a new nation. A nation founded on the principles of faith and freedom. As the kings of the earth sought to control, restrain, and manipulate the revivals sweeping the world, God opened a door for a new beginning.

A Nation is Born

For about one hundred years men had been sailing to the Americas in quest of wealth and fame. They came with the sword, sometimes even in the name of the Lord, to conquer and pillage. They found gold and silver and peoples to enslave. Through conquest they established their little kingdoms. But there was an area that did not capture their attention, for it was not rich with gold and silver but covered with forests.

It was in this area that small groups of settlers finally began to arrive. Most of these groups were not seeking wealth and fame, but they were seeking freedom to live out their faith. Away from kings and princes, traditions and restrictions, these men drew up simple Biblically based charters to govern their settlements. These simple agreements created a pattern that became the foundation for government in the development of the colonies that grew up around them.

Removed from the oversight of oppressive government man's potential became unbridled. Individual freedom restricted only by the Law of God transformed this wild untamed land into thriving colonies. Of course as time progressed the prosperity of the colonies drew the attention of the rest of the world. The combination of equality and freedom created an environment filled with opportunity and potential on a scale unknown in the established countries of the world. Of course this environment had its own peculiar problems, for this country became a magnet for all sorts of characters.

The discovery by Europeans of the Americas opened these vast continents to them for discovery and collision with the societies that had developed apart from them. But the area that later became the United States was unique in all of the many areas of conquest and colonization. So unique was the founding of this nation, that it later became the model that transformed, not only the Americas, but impacted the entire world. The rapid rise of this nation caught the world's attention is such a way that many people in many places tried to mimic it. Despite the popularity of its example it was never duplicated and remained unique of all the nations of the World.

Eventually the United States stretched from sea to sea, but what was spread across this vast land mass began in those few simple settlements on the Atlantic coast. This was only the second time in all of human history that a nation had this unique opportunity to begin new upon a foundation of dedication to God and His Word. Israel of course being that first nation establish upon the Word of God. Now for the first time in three thousand years small groups of pilgrims were freed from the oppression of kings to begin a new nation established on the Word of God.

This small beginning allowed for the development of law as a form of government. These were laws that were agreed upon by the community, rather than laws being imposed upon them from a hierarchy, tradition, or king. There have been other societies that have had this opportunity to a limited degree. But what made this situation unique was that the law that united these people was the law that was handed down to them from God, through Moses, and ratified by Jesus Christ. This law had its foundation in an authority higher than any man on Earth.

It was these simple organizations of Christians that established the foundation of the nation that was to follow. There were business organizations that also tried to establish themselves in this new land. And of course there was the long reach of the kings of Europe. But what had begun by those simple pilgrims had taken root. The freedom and security that was experienced in a God-centered society created benefits for all and created a level playing field. Prosperity came and with it many new challenges.

Revolution?

One hundred and fifty years after the founding of the colonies the trade and interaction between Europe and American had increased dramatically. But it still was a long distance between them. That distance created a real disconnect between those who lived in Europe and those in the American Colonies. Generations of people had grown up in American Colonies that were ever expanding into the frontier. Freedom, self-government, and self-reliance had become a way of life for many of these people. It was the Seven Years War that focused much of

England's attention on the Colonies. The war had been costly and England began to impose taxes to extract more money from the Colonies.

As the tax burden began to fall on the citizens of the Colonies the realities of the great divide between Europe and the Colonies was laid bare. This was much more than the divide of a vast ocean. The common people of the Colonies had, over decades of time, experienced more freedom and equality than anyone of their European cousins. Parliament's referral to the Colonies as plantations and the colonists as subservient individuals struck a nerve in the colonies inciting rebellion.

The usual focus on the rebellion in the Colonies is on the taxes, the economy, and the lack of representation in Parliament. But there was also a push from England to rein in the religious freedom that the colonists had for so long enjoyed. Today we have a hard time imagining how prevalent and influential the church was in the life of the colonists. The resistance message was coming from the pulpit as well as from the pub, and England knew it.

There have been many revolutions and revolutionaries who have used this Revolutionary War as an example and an excuse for their own rebellion. But this revolution was different than most in that it was not an attempt to revolutionize their government and way of life, rather it was a fight to preserve what they had achieved over the last 150 years. The bondage of a strict overseer was bearing down on a society that had experienced the taste of freedom, and it created a firestorm.

Revival

Christianity and the Bible were foundational to many of the early settlements. If we examine the early charters and laws that were enacted in the Colonies it becomes obvious how much influence the Biblical precepts had in fashioning the laws of the land. But as the Colonies developed and prospered these societies became increasingly materialistic and worldly. This is a typical pattern that is evidenced throughout man's history.

In the 1730's revival began stirring in America and Europe. In 1740 George Whitefield visited the Colonies and the ensuing revival swept across them. The effect of this "Great Awakening" was instrumental in setting the stage for the Church's involvement in the quest for independence from England. Stirring up the precepts of the Biblical foundations of the Colonies played a huge role in defining the foundation of the ensuing republic. The justification for rebellion against the King of England was an appeal to higher power, the Creator God and our Lord Jesus Christ. After all, had not the Creator granted to all men unalienable rights that the King had usurped?

Independence

Against all odds those bold men and women that had risked all, appealing to the mercy of the Most High God, were granted independence from England and the kings of Europe. The next few years the Colonies had to grapple with the ramifications of what that meant. Freedom from England did not mean freedom from responsibility. It was obvious that the only way this new nation would survive would be to establish a permanent bond.

It was with this understanding that the Continental Congress met with representatives from the individual Colonies.

The war for independence had brought the Colonies together in a way that spanned their borders. Especially amongst the younger generation they had begun to think of themselves as Americans. But as they came together they came as representatives of their own states. Their purpose in coming together was to draw up a binding agreement to govern their future relationship together. But after a time of partisan squabbling it was beginning to seem impossible. Finally, a senior statesman arose and suggested that they take a break, go to church, and pray for guidance from above. At last there was agreement for something, and they adjourned.

What happened next can only be described as a miracle. When they reconvened, the perspective had dramatically changed, and the document that came out of that meeting created a foundation for this fledgling nation that has preserved us till this day. July 4th 1776 the Colonies had declared their independence from England. But it was the Constitution and its Ratification that took place between 1787 and 1789 that established the United States of America and the rule of Law.

John Adams would later say: "Our Constitution was made only for a moral and religious people. It is wholly inadequate to the government of any other." Looking back people fail to understand what was clearly understood in this day. We may assume that a nation was founded without a king. But that is not entirely true. One of the phrases of the day was: "We will have no king but Jesus". And many of this day viewed Jesus as their king. Their government was the rule of law, outlined in the Constitution and directed by the inspired Word of God. The King of their country would not rule through kings and governors, but through an individual's heart, conscience and the Bible. Morals would be dictated through law and not though dictators. Judgment would be handed down based upon that law and not the whims of tyrants.

Our Constitution was established with checks and balances. Attached was the Bill of Rights defining boundaries of government interference. Yet there was and still remains one great weakness in our system. That weakness is that the ultimate responsibility for maintaining our Republic rests on the heads of its citizens. Our history reveals that as our citizenry strays from the commandments of God, so goes the safeguards of the Nation. Revive the moral atmosphere, and the Nation recovers. We now sit on the precipice of annihilation for we as a nation have lost our moral compass, the Word of God.

A Nation Set Apart

I have set the United States in a unique category as one of two nations that was founded on and established on the Law of God. Today both nations present a very diverse and complicated picture. Yet if we go back to their roots we will see their godly foundations. With Israel it was Abraham, a man who separated himself from his kin and country. At the direction of God he traveled to a foreign land to found a nation and people who would be a testimony of God's grace and mercy. They were a nation that was intended to bring blessing on all the nations of the earth. We all know how this turned out. In spite of Israel's ups and downs God used this nation to fulfill His plan of redemption for mankind through Jesus Christ. Even today Israel's very existence is a testimony of God's mercy and grace.

Likewise, the Pilgrims and likeminded settlers came to the Americas, separating themselves from kin and tradition to found a nation that would bring glory to God. A study of their writings reveals their intent was to build a nation founded upon the Word of God. Their vision was that this Nation would be like a city on a hill, a pattern to be followed, and a blessing to those nations that they had come from.

In many ways their vision has been fulfilled. Every nation on earth has been blessed by what has come forth from the shores of the United States. The prosperity and blessings that we have experienced inspired peoples around the globe to try to emulate the success and rise of our nation. No other nation has been as instrumental in spreading the Gospel of Jesus Christ throughout the world. At times there were those who acknowledged that America had become great because it was good.

But that road to greatness was not always smooth. There are some dark times in our history as America strayed from their righteous roots. It seems like each generation had to face up to their accountability to their foundation. Freedom has its risks. The pilgrims had sought for freedom to live righteously. Wisely they recognized early on that being governed by righteous law was the only way to preserve that freedom.

The miracle of the United States still lies in the blessings that come from heaven above. We have always been a nation separated out of the other nations. God's plan for the United States was to be a blessing to the whole world, and we have been. There has never been a more generous nation than that of the United States. Again, this goes back to our roots, and our foundation in the Holy Scripture.

Pride and Prejudice

"Pride [goeth] before destruction, and an haughty spirit before a fall." (Pr 16:18 AV)

The Scripture is full of knowledge and wisdom. The instructions for peace and happiness are contained within its pages. But there are also warnings about the consequences for violating the laws that govern the Universe. The problem is that if we do not seek wisdom from its pages, then we will not find wisdom. Neglect breeds ignorance. Ignorance breeds foolishness.

Failure to acknowledge the source of our blessings, leads to forgetfulness. A proud and haughty people are those who have forgotten where they came from. And when those blessing have been withdrawn that we have for so long been recipients of, then we are faced with a dilemma; will we humble ourselves, or will we stiffen our neck? Will we appeal to the source of goodness, or will we go down wallowing in our own stinking pride?

It was in the midst of one of the greatest crisis this Nation ever faced that President Lincoln rose up and appealed to the Nation to recognize the source of our difficulty, and that was pride.

"We have been the recipients of the choicest bounties of Heaven. We have been preserved, these many years, in peace and prosperity. We have grown in numbers, wealth and power, as no other nation has ever grown. But we have forgotten God. We have forgotten the gracious hand which preserved us in peace, and multiplied and enriched and strengthened us; and we have vainly imagined, in the deceitfulness of our hearts, that all these blessings were produced by some superior wisdom and virtue of our own. Intoxicated with unbroken success, we have become too self-sufficient to feel the necessity of redeeming and preserving grace, too proud to pray to the God that made us!" Abraham Lincoln

Even in our relatively short history we can see a pattern that reveals the relationship between godly living and heavenly blessing. True morality is based upon the Law of God. Right and wrong are not just ideas, but are based upon the spiritual laws that govern the universe. There are consequences when we violate the physical laws, and there are consequences when we violate the spiritual laws. Pride (that unholy attitude of the heart), when it rises up, deceives us into thinking that for some reason we can rise above the Law and it will not affect us. It took the extreme cataclysmic events of the Civil War for Abraham Lincoln to fully understand this reality. Time has dulled this principle in our thinking since then, but its truth remains.

As a nation we are again in great crisis. This time the crisis is much deeper, for the foundation of our nation has been undermined. The great building blocks of our nation have been compromised. No longer do we as a nation recognize our godly foundation and the reliance upon the blessings of God for our continued existence. We have become a nation of many gods, and many of our people have put their faith in government. Now, in times of crisis the people look to the government, and not toward God.

It seems as if the majority of our population is deluded by illusion. They have been convinced that they are gods. They have assumed authority for determining what is right and wrong. They perceive themselves as an evolved people in an evolved society and have presented a new morality of their own making. Truth is on trial and scores of people have been convinced that truth is relative, that there are no absolutes. Each man is encouraged to live in his own little world, ignoring the ramifications of ignoring reality.

Again, as so often seen in history, pride has lifted its ugly head and serves to blind people to the realities all around them. Pride finds its encouragement in the lies that continue to blind people. They seek refuge in the promises of those who orchestrated the calamities that they face.

CHAPTER 4
From Sin to Redemption

But For the Love of God

"... but from the tree of the knowledge of good and evil you shall not eat, for in the day that you eat from it you will surely die." (Ge 2:17 NAS95)

When people stray from the truth, ignoring the Law of God, there are consequences. God has never withheld the knowledge of what those consequences would be. From the first instance of Man's rebellion against God's Law, Man knew the consequences. So why do people rebel? What compels people to participate in self-destructive behavior? What will it take to wake us up to the inevitable consequences?

I remember one time I was trying to get something from the joists in my barn. In an attempt to get high enough to reach it, I stepped onto something that could not hold my weight. In that split second before I landed on the ground the thought flashed through my brain, "that was sure stupid". In this particular case I did not suffer the full consequences of my foolish actions because a couple of boxes of old newspapers cushioned my fall; nevertheless, I did not repeat my foolish action. I got a ladder for safer access to my goal, thanking God for old newspapers strategically positioned, and mercy.

Honesty was necessary to be protected from a repeat performance that may have had more dire consequence. I had to admit that it was my actions that needed to be adjusted because the law of gravity is not a respecter of persons, and I was not exempt. We need to be honest with ourselves, if we are to take advantage of God's grace and mercy. Just as the ladder was my tool to overcome the law of gravity, what Jesus did for us on the cross is necessary for us to overcome the consequences of the law of sin and death.

The Scripture tells us that all of us have sinned and the consequence of sin is death; however, in the unfolding story of man, we find in the Bible there are two underlying themes, "but God", and "If we will". I fell in my barn, but there was a ladder. If I would have used it, I would not have fallen. Man fell in the Garden of Eden, but God has provided a way of redemption, if we are willing.

How many times the story of Man would have come to an abrupt end had it not been for God's intervention; but for the love of God, but for the grace of God, but for God's mercy that has endured from generation to generation. How often on a personal level, a national level, or as it was in the days of Noah on a global level, would life have ended, but for the love of God.

Honesty

"Then the LORD God said to the woman, "What is this you have done?" And the woman said, "The serpent deceived me, and I ate." (Ge 3:13 NAS95)

> *"Then to Adam He said, "Because you have listened to the voice of your wife, and have eaten from the tree about which I commanded you, saying, 'You shall not eat from it ... "*
> (Ge 3:17 NAS95)

Since we have become the recipients of the knowledge of good and evil, and since we can throughout our history see the consequences of violating the laws that govern the Universe; why do people continue to disregard those laws in spite of the consequences? Are people not repeating the same mistakes that were made in the Garden when Man first sinned?

Eve was deceived by a lie. Adam listened to the voice of his wife. It is clear that their failure came about because they did not trust God. Satan had succeeded in convincing them to question the love of God in spite of the fact that they had no reason to question God. They lacked nothing. The whole earth was given to them. What more could they desire? Satan's lure was to express his own desire that to be like God was something to be achieved. The lie was that God had withheld something from them and they were not truly free.

One bite of the forbidden fruit and they knew that they had been duped. They had failed to trust in the love of God that had provided for them all things. Trusting in the lie had not made them like God nor had it given them freedom. They had indeed lost their freedom and had blemished their likeness to God. Their sin was exposed and they stood naked, fearing the ominous, inevitable meeting with God.

Everything is clear as one stands in the presence of the God of the Universe. Everything is exposed in the light of His presence. The voice of the Serpent is silent. Eve blames the Serpent. Adam blames the woman that God has given him, but God simply addresses their actions. Judgment is imposed because of what each of them has done. The Serpent is cursed. Eve will suffer in childbirth, and is subjected to the rule of her husband. Adam had brought a curse upon the Earth and was bound to a life of sweat and toil.

Adam and Eve had sinned and there were consequences. Standing before God there were no pretenses, nothing was hidden. Even the Serpent was silent. There is no place for hiding, for lies, or for pretense, as one stands in the light of God's presence where everything is revealed in its entirety.

In this winding path, I have brought you up until this point. I am aiming for an honest evaluation of who we are and where we stand. It is only when we are honest with ourselves and God, that we can assess our condition and our standing before God. When all is said and done, what really matters is our standing before God, the Creator of the Universe.

The Fallen State of Mankind

> *"... for all have sinned and fall short of the glory of God,"* (Ro 3:23 NAS95)

Ray Comfort is a street evangelist. Often he will ask people on the street if they are good people. In most cases the person will answer, "Yes, I am a good person." As the conversation progresses, Ray will present them with the Ten Commandments, the Laws of God. Their defense of their "good person" status begins to falter as they confess their violation of God's moral code.

Most people want to be perceived as good people; however, their defense of that status is based upon what they think, or feel, or maybe even what someone else thinks. Their defense falters when it is confronted with the Word of God. If we are honest, we will admit that none of us naturally holds the high moral ground. We all have sinned and violated God's moral standard.

Adam and Eve occupied the high moral ground, for they were created good and were living in harmony with the Law of God. When Satan challenged Eve, questioning her moral standing, Eve folded. She fell for Satan's lie in spite of the fact that she had knowledge of the truth. In essence, she allowed Satan to lure her down from the high ground to defend her status from his level. If she had stood her ground and defended her status from there, she would have simply said, "God has said...".

We were all born in sin, as sin entered the world through one man, Adam. Also, through one man, Jesus Christ, has come redemption from sin. We can through Christ regain the high moral ground, and when we do, we need to stand fast on that ground. From that position we can defend the righteousness that we have found in Christ Jesus.

Regaining the High Ground Through Faith

*"The LORD God made garments of skin
for Adam and his wife, and clothed them."*
(Ge 3:21 NAS95)

God had a plan. Through sacrifice, He provided a covering for Man's exposed nakedness. Man could now regain that moral high ground through faith that was based on the promise of God to provide a way of salvation. This faith is anchored in hope of the restoration of all things. Our faith is revealed through obedience to God's Word.

"By faith Abel offered to God a better sacrifice than Cain, through which he obtained the testimony that he was righteous, God testifying about his gifts, and through faith, though he is dead, he still speaks." (Heb 11:4 NAS)

Adam and Eve had their beginning on the high ground. Because of their sin, mankind must regain that standing. "If we will, we can regain that standing through faith. If we are unwilling as Cain was, then sin waits at the door. In rejecting the path to acceptance, Cain became jealous that his brother had found acceptance. He killed his brother Abel and was banished from the presence of God.

"And Adam had relations with his wife again; and she gave birth to a son, and named him Seth, for, she said, "God has appointed me

another offspring in place of Abel; for Cain killed him." (Ge 4:25 NAS)

Again we see how that it is God who keeps faith and hope alive through the seed of righteousness. The fulfillment of that seed we find in Christ Jesus, who takes away the sins of the world. It is in God's provision that we have a path back to the moral high ground, so that we once again can be in right standing with God. Once again we can be reconciled to our Creator and stand in his presence unashamed.

A New Birth, A New Man

Arriving on the high ground is not a process of a lifetime of striving and climbing. The high ground is achieved by putting our faith in the Lord Jesus Christ. This may be a little hard for us to understand because it is not how our finite minds work. Right standing before God is based upon our being righteous. It is not even based upon our spiritual maturity. Maybe it would be easier to understand, if we viewed righteousness as being clean. Cleanliness is not contingent upon our age. At any age from newborn to aged we can cleanse ourselves from the filth that surrounds us by washing.

> *"Now there was a man of the Pharisees, named Nicodemus, a ruler of the Jews; this man came to Jesus by night and said to Him, "Rabbi, we know that You have come from God [as] a teacher; for no one can do these signs that You do unless God is with him." Jesus answered and said to him, "Truly, truly, I say to you, unless*

one is born again he cannot see the kingdom of God." Nicodemus *said to Him, "How can a man be born when he is old? He cannot enter a second time into his mother's womb and be born, can he?" Jesus answered, "Truly, truly, I say to you, unless one is born of water and the Spirit he cannot enter into the kingdom of God "That which is born of the flesh is flesh, and that which is born of the Spirit is spirit. "Do not be amazed that I said to you, 'You must be born again." (Joh 3:1-7 NAS95)

"Born Again," has become a phrase that is now used in reference to a new beginning, a new way of thinking, or a new direction in our lives. Biblically speaking, it is literally a new birth, not a physical or mental renewing, but a spiritual birth. This birth is the result of our interaction with God's Spirit. God is then the father of this new person. It is only after this takes place that we can actually say that we are the sons of God, because before this we were spiritually dead.

Jesus said we must be born of the water and the Spirit. Nicodemus was obviously struggling to understand what all this meant and how it was to come about.

"For God so loved the world, that he gave his only begotten Son, that whosoever believeth in him should not perish, but have everlasting life." (Joh 3:16 AV)

This verse that so many of us memorized from an early age, really sums up this whole chapter that reveals a foundational understanding of God's plan to reconcile Man unto Himself. I won't take the time here to go verse by verse through this passage, but I want to point out that it is through the water and the Spirit that we receive our new birth.

Later on after Jesus had accomplished his work on the cross, the understanding of how this was to be accomplished was explained. It was on the day of Pentecost that the Spirit of God fell on the disciples in such a way that it could be observed by those around them. This public display created a platform to present the way of salvation to those gathered in Jerusalem. Upon the explanation of the death of Jesus on the cross, and the revelation of the sin of those standing there, they were convicted and cried out, "What must we do?" The answer was that they needed to repent of their sins, be baptized, and then God would fill them with His Spirit.

I think that these instructions are so simple that sometimes people miss the fundamental process that leads to our salvation. We are sinners. The Holy Spirit convicts us of our sin. Godly sorrow brings forth repentance. Through the sacrificial death of Jesus we can be forgiven of our sins. Baptism in water is the testimonial of our being cleansed from all unrighteousness. A clean vessel is now open to the presence of God's Spirit. He fills us and makes us alive through a new birth.

We have just arrived at that high plain, the high moral ground where we are in right standing before God. We are not alone here, but are surrounded with the Saints of all ages. We have become a member of the Church of Jesus Christ. He is the head and we are the body, individual members of this vast assembly of God's children.

A Safe Place

"For I am convinced that neither death, nor life, nor angels, nor principalities, nor things present, nor things to come, nor powers, nor height, nor depth, nor any other created thing, will be able to separate us from the love of God, which is in Christ Jesus our Lord." (Ro 8:38-39 NAS95)

There is no safer place than when we abide in Christ, fully trusting in Him. The process I just explained culminates in a new birth and, spiritually speaking, the person becomes a new babe in Christ. Everybody knows how helpless and vulnerable new babies are. Left to themselves all babies would simply die; however, they do not die because we create a safe space for them. Nestled in our homes in our most favorable environment, we protect and nurture our young ones. Even more important than the place, are the people that surround this babe: the God-designed family of a mother, father, siblings, grandparents, aunts and uncles, to provide a bulwark that stands between this little one and the worldly elements. As it is in the physical, it is even more so in the spiritual. God as our father provides all things for the safety, comfort, and nutritional needs of His little children.

In spite of all that God has done to protect His children there still lies one grave danger, a vulnerability that exists because of who we are. That vulnerability is our will and the ability to choose. This is where Satan attacked in the Garden and this is where the attack comes today. We need to understand where our safety lies. As long as we continue to trust God, there is nothing that can harm us. We are safe, if we keep faith. We acquired the high ground by faith and we remain here by faith.

As we continue this discussion concerning the high ground, I want to keep reminding you that our standing on the moral high ground is not contingent upon our level of spiritual maturity. Neither is it contingent upon any talent that God may bestow upon us, or our expertise at using that talent. Our standing on this place is always based upon our faith and trust in God and His Word.

CHAPTER 5
Growing Up

Growing Up

"So when they had finished breakfast, Jesus
*said to Simon Peter, "Simon, [son] of John,
do you love Me more than these?" He *said
to Him, "Yes, Lord; You know that I love You."
He *said to him, "Tend My lambs." He *said
to him again a second time, "Simon, [son] of
John, do you love Me?" He *said to Him, "Yes,
Lord; You know that I love You." He *said to him,
"Shepherd My sheep." He *said to him the third
time, "Simon, [son] of John, do you love Me?"
Peter was grieved because He said to him the
third time, "Do you love Me?" And he said to
Him, "Lord, You know all things; You know that
I love You." Jesus *said to him, "Tend My sheep."
(Joh 21:15-17 NAS95)

In anticipation of the influx of new births that were to take
place in the days ahead, Jesus began preparing the disciples
for their task ahead. As anyone knows, one of the most basic
needs of babies is milk. Jesus' request of Peter was for him
to feed His lambs. Jesus revealed to us that there is great joy

among the angels of God when one sinner repents; however, that is just the beginning. Once a baby is born, it needs to be fed.

> *"... like newborn babies, long for the pure milk of the word, so that by it you may grow in respect to salvation,"* (1Pe 2:2 NAS95)

The Scripture continually compares our physical birth and growth with our spiritual birth and growth. Milk is so very important in our early development and likewise in our spiritual development. It is in partaking of the pure milk of the Word that the new man begins to grow and develop. When consumed in abundance, the babe experiences rapid and healthy growth. How very important it is at this early stage, for a person to stay close and drink often from the source of this life giving food.

> *"... but whoever causes one of these little ones who believe in Me to stumble, it would be better for him to have a heavy millstone hung around his neck, and to be drowned in the depth of the sea."* (Mt 18:6 NAS95)

The early stages of a person's spiritual life are also a time of great vulnerability. As I have already pointed out, as long as we hold an unwavering faith and trust in Jesus, we remain safe and secure. The young in the faith lack the knowledge and experience to do battle with the voices of the world. The strategy of the enemy is to lure the unsuspecting from their position of safety, which is faith in God. It is, therefore, the responsibility of Christ's Church to build a bulwark around these babes in Christ to protect and counter the attacks that are inevitable. This is an area of weakness in the American Church today. Surrounded by a culture of extreme sensitivity for offenses, the Church has become silent in defending the principles of behavior that provide that bulwark of protection.

There is another danger to the vulnerability of these tender new converts that lies within the church itself. Compromise of the Scriptural teachings and principles by those who profess to be Christians, can be more effective in creating doubt and apprehension than those attacks from the outside. I hope to deal in more detail about some of these compromises later. I raise this issue in the context of spiritual growth because of the important ramifications to the new believer, and for those who inadvertently are providing stumbling blocks.

Striving for Maturity

"For though by this time you ought to be teachers, you have need again for someone to teach you the elementary principles of the oracles of God, and you have come to need milk and not solid food." (Heb 5:12 NAS95)

"Wisdom [is] the principal thing; [therefore] get wisdom: and with all thy getting get understanding." (Pr 4:7 AV)

As the father of four grown children, I have experienced the joys that come with fatherhood. We cherish their achievements and the milestones in their development from their birth, and continuing throughout their lifetime. I have no doubt that it is the same with our heavenly Father.

The Scripture tells us that there is great joy in all of heaven at the birth of one of God's children. It is also clear that God's desire for all of His children is for them to continue to develop and mature. God's goal and purpose is that we continue to grow spiritually, conforming to the image of His only begotten son, Christ Jesus.

More than once the Apostle Paul expresses disappointment that some of God's children were a little slow in growing up. In the passage quoted above, it seems like some were actually reverting back to their childish ways to the extent that they were in need of having to be taught the basic fundamentals again. In spite of the fact that they were old enough, and should have learned enough to have become teachers, they were yet incapable of understanding anything beyond the most basic truths.

It was not because the milk was not good and essential for our development, that the writer of Hebrews was lamenting the fact that they were not able to eat solid food. It was because God never intended for us to remain babies for the rest of our lives. There was so much more God wanted to share with His children that could not be experienced until they grew up a little. As long as we cannot eat solid food, we are in need of milk. If we are in this condition, we are still in the need of the direct guidance of a teacher.

Big Babies

"For everyone who partakes [only] of milk is not accustomed to the word of righteousness, for he is an infant. But solid food is for the mature, who because of practice have their senses trained to discern good and evil." (Heb 5:13-14 NAS95)

The maturing process requires exercise and practice to develop our senses, training us by the Word of God to be able to discern good and evil. Failure to partake of the Word of God, and to receive training in righteousness, results in retardation.

It seems like in America today, there is an epidemic of retardation in many of the churches. People who have been "Christians" for years, seem to be ignorant of the most basic principles of the teachings of Christ. The Scriptural solution for this dilemma is that they be taught again those fundamental principles of Christ's teachings. In their present condition, they can only handle milk. Instead of being given milk, those who are presiding over these large nurseries seem to find it easier just to give them candy and cool-aid.

We see a trend prevailing in our culture, and in our churches, whereby many people have attained physical maturity, but have retained childish attitudes. Simply put, they are just big babies, expecting someone else to continue to give them everything that they desire. They refuse to take responsibility for their own actions. What we need to understand, if we are to change this trend, is that those in charge of raising these children are often the ones at fault. In our culture, the blame lies with the parents and educators. In the church, it is the same. Those who are responsible for the nurturing and educating of young Christians, have not fulfilled their responsibility. Usually this means that for the most part, they have taken the easy route. It is easier to provide entertainment than education. It is easier to feed candy and cool-aid than it is to ensure a diet of adequate nutrition. It is easier to let children have their own way than it is to provide discipline and correction. When we end up with big babies, it becomes obvious that the easy way was not the best way. Big babies are harder to deal with than newborn babies.

Now What?

So, what do you do if you end up with a bunch of big babies? The answer is clear in our passage from Hebrews 5:12. The big babies need to be taught again the elementary principles of the oracles of God. It sounds simple, but it is not easy because these are not new infants. They are people in whom the maturing process has not gone well. Although we cannot go back in time, we have the instruction that Paul gave to Timothy, that seems applicable to this situation.

> *"Flee also youthful lusts: but follow righteousness, faith, charity, peace, with them that call on the Lord out of a pure heart. But foolish and unlearned questions avoid, knowing that they do gender strifes. And the servant of the Lord must not strive; but be gentle unto all [men], apt to teach, patient, In meekness instructing those that oppose themselves; if*

God peradventure will give them repentance
to the acknowledging of the truth; And [that]
they may recover themselves out of the snare
of the devil, who are taken captive by him at
his will." (2Ti 2:22-26 AV)

Immaturity in people who's "senses haven't been trained to discern good and evil", creates a tendency to ask "foolish and unlearned questions". Paul instructs Timothy not to fight or argue with them. Instead, we are to gently teach the truth with patience and meekness, to this group that is in opposition to themselves. We need to understand that they are in the need of repentance, because they have fallen into the snare of the devil. It says here in Scripture that they have been taken captive by the devil at his will. This would imply that they have strayed from the safety and protection of that high ground.

Continuing to Strive for Maturity

"Therefore leaving the elementary teaching
about the Christ, let us press on to maturity, not
laying again a foundation of repentance from
dead works and of faith toward God," (Heb
6:1 NAS95)

"Not that I have already obtained [it] or have
already become perfect, but I press on so that
I may lay hold of that for which also I was laid
hold of by Christ Jesus. Brethren, I do not regard
myself as having laid hold of [it] yet; but one
thing [I do:] forgetting what [lies] behind and

> *reaching forward to what [lies] ahead, I press*
> *on toward the goal for the prize of the upward*
> *call of God in Christ Jesus."* (Php 3:12-14 NAS95)

God's purpose for His children is for them to become con-
formed to the image of His Son, Jesus Christ. God's goal for us
should be our goal for ourselves. What this means is that we
have a whole lot of growing up to do. In Peter's epistle, we are
told that we were born of holy seed. Our new birth was an act
of God. This is what makes us His children and He becomes our
Father. From the moment of our new birth, we were created
in His likeness and image. If there was no resemblance, even
from this early point in our life, we might question whether we
were truly His child.

It is true that we may start out as a very immature image of
God; nevertheless, the offspring of the God of love better be full
of love. The mature image of love we see in Christ is revealed
in His sacrificial death on the cross, on our behalf. In Christ, we
see the perfection or mature image of what we are destined
to become.

If the apostle Paul was still pressing toward that mark in the
latter days of his ministry, then it is way too early for us to settle
for something short of what God would have for us. As I have
already mentioned, maturing is not just about getting older, but
it is about developing the extent of our capabilities. What we
end up individually looking like will in some ways vary, but it
will invariably be an expression of the love of God.

There may be times or reasons why we might want to stop this whole maturing process. There certainly is in the spiritual, just like in the physical, such a thing as growing pains. There is a lot more to maturity than just getting bigger. We have to have instruction, correction, and everything else involved in education. We have to exercise and practice to develop skills and develop endurance. Then in graduated degrees, we have to accept responsibility and responsibilities. There also needs to be as we go along a broadening of the vision of our purpose and goals. Glimpses of future potentials will at times inspire us, and at times may overwhelm us.

This life in Christ also has its sweet spots and there will always be the temptation to just stop and stay right there in a sweet spot. For some, this time comes as early as when they first come to Christ, drink of the milk, share in the fellowship, and just enjoy being babied. For some of us we may desire to go back to a simpler time when we were less aware of the evil around us, and were not feeling the heaviness of responsibility weighing down on us. The realities of life do not allow for us to stop or go back. Whether we are talking about the physical or the spiritual, we need to press on ahead. To stop is to stagnate, from there we go downhill, and then eventually we will die.

It is important that we press on in this high calling in Christ Jesus. We soon realize that it is not just about us. We are here to help others along the way. We also find that there are those who are called to help us along our way. Our path of development will either make it harder or easier for those who follow us. Keeping our eyes fixed on Jesus as we press on is essential, if we are to maintain our standing on the high ground.

Saints, the Faithful in Christ

"Paul, an apostle of Jesus Christ by the will of God, to the saints which are at Ephesus, and to the faithful in Christ Jesus: Grace [be] to you, and peace, from God our Father, and [from] the Lord Jesus Christ." (Eph 1:1-2 AV)

Paul's letter to the Ephesians starts with a greeting that is typical in all his letters. The term, "saint", in our present day is usually only used for those who have passed on and have been elevated to a special level. But the term "saint" simply means "holy one". Those who are truly Christians, have had their sins washed away, and are living lives faithful to Christ today, simply are the saints of God. This is not a status that is achieved by accomplishing great deeds or the high acclaim of men, rather it is a position that we obtain through repentance and the forgiveness of sins. We are then obligated and inspired through love and thanksgiving to God to walk worthy of this calling. We accomplish this by putting our trust in Jesus as our Savior and in the power of God's Spirit that dwells within us to live a holy life before God and man.

Those who are saints are to be the light of the world. We are to be the salt of the earth. We are to be the witnesses of the love of God that came to earth to save people from sin and death. That is why I have spent time here emphasizing the importance of God's children maturing in their faith. That is why God had the apostle Paul instruct the saints in all the Churches, preparing them for the role that the Church has in every generation. That is why we cannot cede our standing on the moral high ground, that place of right standing with God. It is only by being positioned on the high moral ground that we can shine the light of the gospel effectively.

Apostles, Prophets, and Teachers

"And He gave some [as] apostles, and some [as] prophets, and some [as] evangelists, and some [as] pastors and teachers, for the equipping of the saints for the work of service, to the building up of the body of Christ; until we all attain to the unity of the faith, and of the knowledge of the Son of God, to a mature man, to the measure of the stature which belongs to the fullness of Christ. As a result, we are no longer to be children, tossed here and there by waves and carried about by every wind of doctrine, by the trickery of men, by craftiness in deceitful scheming; but speaking the truth in love, we are to grow up in all [aspects] into Him who is the head, [even] Christ," (Eph 4:11-15 NAS95)

Again, I want to emphasize that a person's standing on the high ground and the title of saint, are not contingent upon our level of maturity. It is simply based upon our right standing before God. It is not based upon our understanding of the principles of God, but our acceptance of them as a guide for our lives. It is not based upon our level of knowledge or wisdom, but upon our trust in Jesus and the Word of God.

But how we are positioned on that high ground may be based upon some of these things. Our maturity and personal gifts come into play when we consider what God is asking us as individuals to do. God doesn't put his babies in the middle of the battlefield. He does not require those still reliant upon a diet of milk to serve meat. He does not ask children to be teachers.

I think you can get my point from these few examples. God prepares us for the tasks that lie before us. David killed a bear and a lion before he needed to stand up in front of a giant. God's provisions come in many ways and forms. Our abilities, gifts, and opportunities come from God. But there is an element that lies strictly in our hands and that is our willingness. God looks for a person who is willing. When we place ourselves in God's hand, then He can provide us with the knowledge, wisdom, and abilities necessary to perform His will.

> *"And Jesus said to them, "Follow Me, and I will make you become fishers of men." Immediately they left their nets and followed Him."* (Mr 1:17-18 NAS95)

Apostles, prophets, evangelists, and pastors and teachers, are men of God's making. These are men who have responded to the call of God and followed Jesus. These are men who are patterning their lives after their teacher and guide. These are men who have reached a level of maturity in which they can be used of God to lead, guide, exhort, and teach. Their position is not based upon their level of maturity or their desire for a particular position, but the calling of God in their lives. We are asked to follow Jesus. It is Jesus who makes us to become an instrument to be used by Him.

These individuals are necessary to guide and lead the followers of Christ on their path to maturity. It is the responsibility of these men is to maintain the purity of the Word of God and equip the saints for the work of the Church. It is the responsibility of these men to build up the body of Christ, maintaining unity with a focus on Christ. If they are successful, followers of Christ will not remain as children that are easily led astray and vulnerable to the cunning deceptions of the devil.

How do you counter false prophets and teachers? You counter them with the truth, the Word of God. That is why we need to recognize how very important it is that we have the knowledge that is contained in God's Word. It is through the Word that we are able to recognize that which is false. It is through the teaching of the Word that God's children are equipped and protected against that which would destroy us.

We become vulnerable when we trust in our own understanding. The warnings are clear that appearances can be deceiving. Wolves in sheep's clothing, signs and wonders, or any of the other deceptive means Satan uses will not sway us from the truth if we adhere to the Word of God. We all need to be students of the Word of God if we are to avoid the threats of false information that can lead us astray. Spiritual maturity does not remove the need for vigilance. The subtle deceptive attacks just come in different ways and on different levels. God's Word provides us with adequate protection as outlined in the 6th chapter of Ephesians, but we have to make use of that armor to be protected.

The role of the teacher is very important in the matters of our spiritual well-being. We also begin to understand the weight of responsibility that falls on those who have been called to teach. It is important that we get it right and closely adhere to the pure unadulterated Word of God. It is not only in what is said, but each one of us have responsibility for the way in which we walk.

A War for Men's Souls

We are in a war and the battle is for the souls of men. Just because we occupy the high moral ground does not mean we will not come under attack. In fact it is because we occupy the high ground that we will be the focus of attacks. What I am trying to show here is that God provides everything we need and equips us to be able to repel any and every attack from the enemy.

I do not want to in any way detract from the concept that I earlier presented. The understanding that even babies are safe and secure from the enemy by their standing on the high ground is still true. But this security is contingent upon their trust in Jesus. The enemy's attacks often come in the form of doubts or enticements. These are the kinds of things that need to be deflected and dealt with by those who are more mature and knowledgeable. One who is still a child may not have the knowledge and understanding to do battle with those who wage war. But as long as they trust God and His Word they cannot be dragged from their position on the high ground.

Protection For Those On The High Ground

"I solemnly charge [you] in the presence of God and of Christ Jesus, who is to judge the living

and the dead, and by His appearing and His kingdom: preach the word; be ready in season [and] out of season; reprove, rebuke, exhort, with great patience and instruction. For the time will come when they will not endure sound doctrine; but [wanting] to have their ears tickled, they will accumulate for themselves teachers in accordance to their own desires, and will turn away their ears from the truth and will turn aside to myths." (2Ti 4:1-4 NAS95)

God has in every generation given a charge to maturing members of the faith and equipped them to preach His Word. It is His Word, whether given as instruction, encouragement, correction, or a rebuke, that guard the safety of those occupying the high ground. When the time comes that people will no longer pay attention to the voice of God through His servants they become vulnerable to the attacks of the enemy. The nature of that attack is to appeal to the lust of the flesh, the lust of the eye, and the pride of life. Subtly those attacks create doubts, questioning the wisdom of God.

How very important it is that those who are more mature continue to seek wisdom and understanding to fulfill their responsibility to guard and deflect the attacks of the enemy. As I view the landscape of America today I see those brave individuals that have taken this charge seriously and are standing firm. They have taken up the armor of God and are preaching His Word with boldness. But I am also aware that we live in a time that many are not willing to endure sound doctrine, but desiring to have their ears tickled they are following false teachers. Safety has been compromised and many churches are crumbling under the attack of the enemy.

False Prophets and Teachers

"Beware of the false prophets, who come to you in sheep's clothing, but inwardly are ravenous wolves." (Mt 7:15 NAS95)

"For false Christs and false prophets will arise and will show great signs and wonders, so as to mislead, if possible, even the elect." (Mt 24:24 NAS95)

"Wherefore I take you to record this day, that I [am] pure from the blood of all [men]. For I have not shunned to declare unto you all the counsel of God. Take heed therefore unto yourselves, and to all the flock, over the which the Holy Ghost hath made you overseers, to feed the church of God, which he hath purchased with his own blood. For I know this, that after my departing shall grievous wolves enter in among you, not sparing the flock." (Ac 20:26-29 AV)

Danger From Within

"... but whoever causes one of these little ones who believe in Me to stumble, it would be better for him to have a heavy millstone hung around

> *his neck, and to be drowned in the depth of the
> sea."* (Mt 18:6 NAS95)

Probably the greatest dangers that Christians face today are the ones that come from within our ranks. False prophets and false teachers can infiltrate our churches and cause much damage. But even a more sinister danger is when one of our own strays from the truth and others naively follow. This is serious business when we consider the potential effect our words and actions can have on others.

It does not seem to be fair that it takes a whole lot of good to offset a little bit of evil. But that is the nature of good and evil. If something is tainted with evil it simply is not good. That is why purity is emphasized in the Scripture. Doctrinal teaching needs to come directly from the Scripture, for true wisdom comes from above.

> *"Let not many [of you] become teachers, my
> brethren, knowing that as such we will incur a
> stricter judgment."* (Jas 3:1 NAS95)

Those who are gifted and obtain a position as a teacher incur a great responsibility because of the extent of their influence. As we think of those men who lead large congregations, or men whose teachings form the doctrinal basis for entire denominations, it is easy to imagine the damage that can be done if they teach in error. James seems to be addressing those who are or wish to be teachers at this level. There are men in every generation who because of their abilities and position exercise great influence over how people will understand the Scripture.

If these men have not come under the tutelage of the Holy Spirit or if in their pride they stray from the purity of the Word, they will incur a strict judgment.

The epistle of James goes on to illustrate the influence of a teacher. By likening a teacher to the bit in a horse's mouth, or the rudder of a ship, we can see how the influence of that small member can turn the whole. A small bit in a horse's mouth determines the direction that horse travels. Likewise, it is the relatively small rudder of a ship that determines its direction. So it is also true that a teacher, just one individual member, can lead a whole congregation in the direction of his teaching.

We also need to realize that all of us in some measure have been entrusted with teaching on some level. As we mature in the faith we inherit a responsibility for those who may be following us. For fathers and mothers their children come first in that line of those who are influenced by their words and behavior. We can and should be good examples to follow. But in all humility we need to use our influence to redirect people's attention toward the example of Christ Himself. After all, Christianity in its purest form is simply discipleship of Christ.

There is grave danger when those who have begun a good walk with the Lord become prideful and stray from sound doctrine. It is not just their own soul that is in danger, for because of their sphere of influence, especially among the immature and the naive, the souls of many are endangered. Those who have become teachers and leaders in their own communities have a grave responsibility to guide those who follow in the path of righteousness. When the leaders stumble it is possible that many people will be affected. But every one of us has a sphere of influence, and we would be wise to consider that our words and actions have consequences. If you cause even one of these little ones to stumble, *"it would be better for* you *to have a heavy millstone hung around his neck, and to be drowned in the depth of the sea."* (Mt 18:6 NAS95)

Where We Stand

I have tried to lay out a basic understanding of where we are as Christians today here in America. I will give a brief recap of what I have said. Briefly I have touched on the history of Christianity and how it has been instrumental in the formation of the United States. I have touched on some of the elements that are essential to understanding our position in Christ as we stand before God. I have touched on how we can achieve a right standing before God, and how important it is for us to maintain that standing. I have labeled "our standing before God" as the "high moral ground". I have touched on the challenges that have come against those who stand on that high moral ground, starting with Adam and Eve in the Garden. As I move on I want to increasingly focus on the issues that we are facing today in America. Maintaining our standing on the "high moral ground" is not a matter of comparing ourselves to the standing of other people. Our standing in this position is a matter of our salvation. Unless we have this standing before God, we will not be saved and will perish with the world.

CHAPTER 6
Justification and Defense

Defending Our Position

I have tried to clearly define the high moral ground. Our standing in this position is wholly contingent upon our reliance on the Word of God. It is our faith in God's Word that allows us to share the eternal truths and the wisdom that has come to us from above. Other people around us may not be aware of the source of our knowledge. Their perception of what we say and who we are could offend them, because our speech and actions will be in conflict with their world view.

I remember a friend of mine making this statement to me: "How come you always win our arguments?" I was taken aback and did not know what to say. I had not been aware that I had won any arguments. We had come together because we had both been drafted into the army. At that time, he had not been a Christian very long; whereas, I had grown up in a Christian home and my father was a minister. Our common faith had drawn us together and we had a lot of discussion about it. He was much more intelligent than I was and more educated. It was not that I was winning the arguments; it was the truths I presented from the Scripture that were convincing him of truth.

There is a danger of becoming prideful and we need to guard against it; however, we cannot allow ourselves to be intimidated by those who would accuse us of being proud. We need to stand for truth and righteousness and live righteously, knowing that it is God who judges the intent of the heart. We who are recipients of the truth need to declare it and make clear its source.

Judge Not

*"Do not judge so that you will not be judged.
"For in the way you judge, you will be judged;
and by your standard of measure, it will be
measured to you."* (Mt 7:1-2 NAS95)

This is one of those Biblical concepts that has suffered much misunderstanding and often complete distortion. I will not take the time here to go into a complete study of this subject, but it is important that we clarify some basics when it comes to judging. Simply put, God is the judge and He has given all judgment over to the Son. That means it is not for us to judge, right? Trust me on this one, we will be much better off if we leave the judging to Him.

A problem arises, because most people do not seem to know what the Bible means when it instructs us not to judge. The distortion of this concept has been used as a club by the enemy to stifle the voice of Christians. The Christian has been called to reveal to the world the judgments of God.

Judgment is twofold. First, it is the determination of right and wrong. God alone is the one who holds this authority. Secondly, judgment is the determination of the consequences of sin. This also is God's determination, not ours. This is not to say that we are to remain ignorant on these matters. On the contrary, God wants us to understand His determinations. From verses that I have already mentioned, we learn that discernment between right and wrong comes with maturity and our receiving instruction from God's Word. We know from the Scripture that the consequence of sin is death. It is only through the blood of Jesus Christ that we are rescued from that death.

God has revealed His judgments, and we are to be witnesses of these truths to the world. Our first responsibility is to live according to His determination of righteousness. Secondly, we are responsible to teach His righteousness. Thirdly, God has delegated authority to those in the family, the Church, and the governments, who hold positions of authority to carry out His judgments, to maintain order and promote righteousness.

Temporal Authority

"Every person is to be in subjection to the governing authorities. For there is no authority except from God, and those which exist are established by God. Therefore whoever resists authority has opposed the ordinance of God; and they who have opposed will receive condemnation upon themselves. For rulers are not a cause of fear for good behavior, but for evil. Do you want to have no fear of authority? Do what is good and you will have praise from the same; for it is a minister of God to you for

good. But if you do what is evil, be afraid; for it does not bear the sword for nothing; for it is a minister of God, an avenger who brings wrath on the one who practices evil. Therefore it is necessary to be in subjection, not only because of wrath, but also for conscience' sake." (Ro 13:1-5 NAS95)

God has delegated some temporal authority for the purpose of maintaining order here on earth. There are authorities both to govern nations and to govern the Church. There is also delegated authority even down to the level of the family. God is a God of order and not of confusion.

Now we all know that the governments of this world are often not that righteous. They have their laws, their courts, and their judgments. Those holding positions of authority have their responsibility. They will eventually have to give an account of how they exercised that authority. Our response and responsibility as believers, is not contingent upon how anyone else fulfills their responsibility. God will have the final judgment and He alone determines right from wrong. We are instructed as Christians to honor those authorities and live peaceable lives.

If perchance those in authority require of us an action that is in violation of the Law of God, then it is our duty to take a stand as Peter and the Disciples did and say, "We must obey God rather than men." Man's law does not usurp God's Law. There will come a time when the kingdoms of this world will become the Kingdom of our Lord. Until then, we live in their world, but we live by God's Law.

Our Defense

"FOR THE EYES OF THE LORD ARE TOWARD THE RIGHTEOUS, AND HIS EARS ATTEND TO THEIR PRAYER, BUT THE FACE OF THE LORD IS AGAINST THOSE WHO DO EVIL." Who is there to harm you if you prove zealous for what is good? But even if you should suffer for the sake of righteousness, [you are] blessed. AND DO NOT FEAR THEIR INTIMIDATION, AND DO NOT BE TROUBLED, but sanctify Christ as Lord in your hearts, always [being] ready to make a defense to everyone who asks you to give an account for the hope that is in you, yet with gentleness and reverence;" (1Pe 3:12-15 NAS95)

Who is there to harm you, if you prove zealous for what is good? The answer of course is those who do evil. You may wonder why we would suffer for righteousness, if the Lord is for us and attending to our prayers. A study of Peter's epistle brings great clarity to this issue. As disciples of Christ, we have been entrusted with the fulfillment of His mission, to offer salvation to everyone who is willing.

We have just considered the fact that Christ will judge all things. If we are in right standing, occupying the high moral ground, then Christ is our defense before the Judge. When we are considering presenting a defense to people, it is not for the purpose of the consideration of their judgments or opinions. Our defense before them is to testify of our faith and confidence that we have in our Lord Jesus Christ. They need to know why we are more concerned about them than we are about ourselves. We need to equip ourselves with answers. Our defense is always rooted in love. Love is our motivation to share with them and try to persuade them to look to Jesus as the source of life.

By sanctifying the Christ as Lord in our hearts, we overcome their attempts to cause us to fear or to be intimidated. Instead, with the love of God in our hearts, we are able to face our persecutors with their well-being in mind and not ours; being always ready to gently and respectfully share this great hope that dwells within us.

Being always ready implies being prepared. Remember we are in a battle here, but our battle is not against flesh and blood. Our battle is against that which enslaves the souls of people. If we do battle correctly, we will have the advantage. We will occupy the high ground. We have been given instruction to equip ourselves and to be encouraged that our strength comes from the Lord. We are told to take a stand and that we stand for truth and righteousness.

Equipped

"Finally, be strong in the Lord and in the strength of His might. Put on the full armor of God, so that you will be able to stand firm against the schemes of the devil. For our struggle is not against flesh and blood, but against the rulers, against the powers, against the world forces of this darkness, against the spiritual [forces] of wickedness in the heavenly [places.] Therefore,

take up the full armor of God, so that you will be able to resist in the evil day, and having done everything, to stand firm. Stand firm therefore, HAVING GIRDED YOUR LOINS WITH TRUTH, and HAVING PUT ON THE BREASTPLATE OF RIGHTEOUSNESS, and having shod YOUR FEET WITH THE PREPARATION OF THE GOSPEL OF PEACE; in addition to all, taking up the shield of faith with which you will be able to extinguish all the flaming arrows of the evil [one.] And take THE HELMET OF SALVATION, and the sword of the Spirit, which is the word of God. With all prayer and petition pray at all times in the Spirit, and with this in view, be on the alert with all perseverance and petition for all the saints," (Eph 6:10-18 NAS95)

Paul's epistle to the Ephesians begins by greeting them as saints (holy ones). As the letter unfolds, we see how we as Christians (the saints) are positioned in the family of God. We are reminded of who we were and where God has brought us to. We are encouraged to grow up and become established in the righteousness of God. We are taught proper relationships one with another. Finally, we are confronted with the conflict that continues to war against our souls. We have been given what is necessary for the battles that lie before us. Now we need to put on that armor so that we will have full protection.

Before we start swinging our swords, we need to understand what we are up against and know who the enemy is. Our enemy is the devil, and his scheming attacks on us, God's children. Our struggle is not against flesh and blood. This does not mean that there are not going to be people fighting against us, but our struggle is against the forces that have enslaved them. Christ came to redeem man from the clutches of sin. Satan (the devil) has purposed to thwart God's plan of redemption. Satan is no match for God in any way.

> *"You are from God, little children, and have overcome them; because greater is He who is in you than he who is in the world."* (1Jo 4:4 NAS95)

We obtained our standing in Christ through faith. It is also faith that is required for us to maintain our standing. If we stand firm in the Word of God, then nothing can harm us; however, the warning that comes here is that the devil is scheming to undermine our confidence in our Lord Jesus Christ and His power to save us. As we grow in grace and the knowledge of our Lord, we become a threat to the scheming of the devil. Not only are we becoming less vulnerable, but we become a bulwark of protection for those who are coming behind us.

As babes we could be content, surrounded by the fellow believers, to drink of the milk of God's Word, and enjoy the pleasures of peace with God. As we mature in the faith, God asks us to gradually take on responsibilities concerning the Kingdom. We may not end up on the very front line of the battle like the Apostle Paul, but Paul, as a seasoned soldier, wanted us to know that we cannot withstand the schemes of the devil on any level without the armor that God has provided for us. This is not a physical battle, but a spiritual battle. The armor must be spiritual.

The Equipment

Stand firm therefore, HAVING GIRDED YOUR LOINS WITH TRUTH, and HAVING PUT ON THE BREASTPLATE OF RIGHTEOUSNESS, and having shod YOUR FEET WITH THE PREPARATION OF THE GOSPEL OF PEACE; in addition to all, taking up the shield of faith with which you will be able to extinguish all the flaming arrows of the evil [one.] And take THE HELMET OF SALVATION, and the sword of the Spirit, which is the word of God. (Eph. 6: 13–17 NAS95)

Even here in the 21st century, we have a basic understanding of the armor a soldier dons as he goes out to battle. Today, that armor may be more sophisticated, but the images of days gone by have been preserved through stories and traditions. Even though the battles we are considering are spiritual in nature, the principles still remain. Potentially we have vulnerable areas that need to be guarded. God has provided the equipment, but we need to put it on, test it, and get used to wearing it. This armor is not strictly for defense, but also to be used offensively.

Girdle

Stand firm having girded your loins with truth. If you have ever watched a man try to carry a heavy load with both arms while wearing low riding pants without a belt, then maybe you can understand the importance of girding your loins. As his pants slip lower, they not only expose him, but also impede his prog-ress. Clothing is our first line of defense. Although it is not men-tioned here, it is implied by the need to be girded. Clothing needs to be held in the place it was intended to be; otherwise, it can end up being a hindrance to our movements.

We are looking at a physical illustration here to help us understand the importance of preparation for spiritual battles. Let us not lose sight that the realities of the spiritual world are just as real as in the physical world. When we consider that we are girdled with truth, then we begin to visualize that the fundamental precept that ties everything in place is truth. Uncompromising truth is essential to enable us to stand and move with confidence. Once we deviate from truth, we have lost the high ground. Girded with truth, we can face our foe straight on. We cannot battle as our enemy does through conniving and deceptive maneuvering, because we stand for truth and honesty. When we stand girded with truth, we will have the backing of heaven above and can stand in the strength of God's might.

Breastplate

Having put on the breastplate of righteousness, we provide protection for our body and our essential organs. Most important is the guarding of the heart. Spiritually speaking, the heart is central to who we are. This is the seat of our desires. As a Christian, we have been born again, and have been given spiritual insight from the Word of God. Having tasted of this heavenly manna, our hearts desire those things that only God can provide; peace, love, and fellowship with Him. As I ponder the ramifications of this train of thought, it seems to make perfect sense that the armor guarding my heart would be righteousness.

Sometimes we use the words truth and righteousness as being synonymous, but righteousness is more about the way in which we use truth. Righteousness is "rightly using truth". Truth can be manipulated to create a heart of stone. The enemy is not ignorant of the truth. If he can trick us into desiring to be seen as right, then our heart becomes vulnerable and our desires compromised. If we are protected with the breastplate of righteousness, then our godly desires remain intact.

Righteousness protects the heart that is in a life bound by truth. Our breastplate is obtained by grace through faith in the work of Jesus Christ on the cross. It is maintained by the power of God in our lives as we follow Jesus. Christ is our righteousness. With the knowledge of sin came the truths of forgiveness, mercy, and grace, that we might be sanctified and redeemed by His holy blood. Only His righteousness can guard our heart against the pride or the discouragement the enemy would bring.

> *"But by His doing you are in Christ Jesus, who became to us wisdom from God, and righteousness and sanctification, and redemption, so that, just as it is written, "LET HIM WHO BOASTS, BOAST IN THE LORD."* (1Co 1:30-31 NAS95)

Footwear

Our feet are shod with the preparation of the Gospel of Peace. This is not what the enemy wants to see. He would rather see us coming forth with hate and revenge, but we have been informed that our struggle is not against flesh and blood. We have been equipped with preparations of good news that can redeem even those in the service of our enemy.

It is these shoes that present us with a constant reminder of what our mission really is. These shoes provide understanding (pun intended) of why we are willing to face the enemy, and why he is so opposed to our going forth. The world and its inhabitants lie in bondage to sin and corruption. We stand as witnesses of salvation and the good news of deliverance and reconciliation of man to God.

> *"How lovely on the mountains Are the feet of him who brings good news, Who announces peace And brings good news of happiness, Who announces salvation, And says to Zion, "Your God reigns!""" (Isa 52:7 NAS95)*

Shield

Above all, take up the shield of faith. Faith is our confidence in Jesus Christ and the Word of God. Remember that we are talking about Biblical faith. The world's definition of faith amounts to no more than wishful thinking. For them, acting in faith is merely a bold recklessness; however, our faith is confidence in the most reliable person in the universe, God the faithful. Our faith is established by the knowledge of our Lord and Savior Jesus Christ. When we act in faith, we are trusting in the reliability that set the universe in motion.

The shield of faith is necessary because the enemy is shooting flaming arrows at us and this shield will extinguish them. The

King James version of the Scriptures uses the words "fiery darts", or as some have identified them, as "fiery doubts". There are few things that can be as debilitating as doubts. Satan's attack on Eve in the Garden, was to create doubt concerning God and His Word. Doubts are raised about His love for us, His purpose, and if or why He loves us. Doubts are raised concerning our salvation, our sanctification, our justification, or why God would care about us as individuals.

Those doubts easily find traction, if we allow ourselves to focus on our limited abilities or our failure and shortcomings. It is only the shield of faith, that confidence in the faithfulness of our redeemer, that can extinguish those fiery doubts and allow us to stand strong in the might of our Lord and Savior.

Helmet

Then there is the helmet of Salvation. We had better not leave our head unprotected. Most of our sensory perception comes through our head. Sight, hearing, taste, and feeling, are all located here facing up our mind, or control center. As we perceive life from within the protection of our salvation, we have a different perspective of the world around us. You might say, "We can now keep our head on straight."

As we consider the head and its importance, we need to remember that this is the area where others are looking. Our head is associated with our identity, who we are, and what we stand for. The helmet we wear identifies who or what we represent. Our helmet carries the identity of the kingdom we belong to and the King that we serve.

Sword

Then there is the sword. This is not just any sword, but the sword of the Spirit, which is the Word of God. This is what we have been equipped with to engage the enemy. It is also a very versatile piece of equipment. It can cleanly divide that which is good from that which is evil. The broadside can be used to rebuff those who need correction. The sword's very appearance serves as a warning for those who would challenge us. It goes before us clearing the way.

There is no better example of how the sword is used, or its effectiveness, than when we see how Jesus used it. When he was confronted with Satan, He used the Word (sword). He confronted temptation with the Word. When questioned concerning righteousness, godliness, judgment, or authority, He always answered with the Word. Everything He did or said was based upon the Word.

The sword's power is limitless in God's hand, but God has also placed it in our hands. In our hands, it is limited by our ability to wield it. That ability comes as we study and practice the proper use and care of this powerful sword. This sword was designed for one purpose only, and that is to promote and perform the will of God. We need to keep this in mind, for misuse can cause much damage.

Let us not forget that this is the sword of the Spirit. Power to wield the sword is present only in the believer, for the Spirit of God only resides within those who are the redeemed. We are given the sword in our hand, but the power to wield it resides in the Spirit.

Prayer

"With all prayer and petition pray at all times in the Spirit, and with this in view, be on the alert with all perseverance and petition for all the saints," (Eph 6:18 NAS95)

God did not just equip us and then say, off you go. Communication is essential for us to stay on track. Prayer is our connection with God to give us direction, help, supplies, and inspiration. Many a general has learned the hard way not to outdistance their supply line, or miss their intelligence briefings. Prayer is our constant reminder of our dependence upon God, and that we are not alone. Prayer is used here in the Scripture in its broadest sense, not just the act of asking for something, but all prayers and petitions.

It is our connection with God that helps us maintain the proper perspective. It also broadens that perspective as we are encouraged to be on the alert. It is easy to become shortsighted and let our guard down; however, as we take to heart this admonition to petition also for all the saints, we are reminded that we are not the only ones facing struggles. The battle is much bigger than we can see right in front of our eyes, and we need to remain alert and persevere.

CHAPTER 7
Foundational Law

A Nation Forsakes God

"The people served the LORD all the days of Joshua, and all the days of the elders who survived Joshua, who had seen all the great work of the LORD which He had done for Israel. Then Joshua the son of Nun, the servant of the LORD, died at the age of one hundred and ten. And they buried him in the territory of his inheritance in Timnath-heres, in the hill country of Ephraim, north of Mount Gaash. All that generation also were gathered to their fathers; and there arose another generation after them who did not know the LORD, nor yet the work which He had done for Israel. Then the sons of Israel did evil in the sight of the LORD and served the Baals, and they forsook the LORD, the God of their fathers, who had brought them out of the land of Egypt, and followed other gods from among the gods of the peoples who were around them, and bowed themselves down to them; thus they provoked the LORD to anger. So they forsook the LORD and served Baal and the Ashtaroth." (Jud 2:7-13 NAS95)

remember as a child hearing the stories from the Bible about the Children of Israel as God brought them out of slavery and established them in the Land of Israel. As the history of Israel was unfolded to me as I grew up in Sunday school, one predominant thought stuck in my mind. How could an entire nation so dramatically change in one generation from devotion to God to worship of idols? And it was not as if this was a onetime event, but time after time they followed the same pattern. God would miraculously rescue them from their enemies and they would serve Him for a time. But it was not long before they would forsake their covenant with God and begin to serve gods that were the product of man's hand and his imagination.

A child is limited in his understanding because of his limited knowledge and experience. Innocence gives way to reality as we experience life through the years. I am in my 60's as I write this and have a much broader perspective to view the history that is recorded in the Bible. I have experienced my nation turn its back on God and reverse the foundational principles upon which it was founded. Not only has this decline happened all within my generation, but I have been astounded at the speed this downward spiral has taken in just the last few years. How can a nation dramatically blessed by God, reverse course in one generation and forsake God? I have seen the answer to this question in real time as I have witnessed my nation turning from God in my short lifetime.

The United States, like Israel, has experienced the blessings of God that come by living according to the principles revealed in the Scripture. My nation is now following the path of ancient Israel in spite of having the recorded history of Israel as an example. Clearly recorded for us are the consequences and destruction that follows neglecting to live in harmony with the Law of God. In addition we have the voice of the prophets that plead with us to cling to those principles that bring life, peace, and fulfillment. And then we have simple logic that is as basic as two plus two equals four. But what seems to win in the end is that people have a tendency to believe what they want to believe. In other words, it is easier to believe a lie than to face reality. Of course, that only works in people's minds; soon reality overtakes delusions and allusions.

There has never been a time or place in which it has been this easy to live in an alternate reality than it is now, here in the United States. This house of cards will eventually fall and reality will be experienced. We are privileged to have those voices that are calling out to this nation to turn from this path of destruction before it is too late. God has not forsaken this nation; it has forsaken Him. I am burdened for my nation, but even more so for the Church. My writing is an appeal to the Church, that they would regain their faith in the Word of God and its power to change lives. As I continue writing I want us to consider those truths that never change and the only sure foundation on which our faith can stand.

Will the Church Forsake God?

Many of the voices coming out of the Church in America today have compromised the clear and powerful voice of Scripture. They have ceded the high moral ground and chosen to present their case on the present cultural level. In so doing they have put themselves on the same level as the religions of this world.

One of the consequences of this strategy is that it has allowed the free flow of ideals to flow from the world into the Church, compromising its message of truth.

Our nation was established as a Christian Republic. Although some of that structure still remains today, all of its fundamental structures have been compromised. As such it cannot stand for long and already shows the signs of stress and decay.

In the same way Jesus established the Church on heavenly principles. His death on the cross made it possible to once again reconcile man to God. The Gospel that was given to the Church is that everyone that will can be saved and obtain eternal life through Christ Jesus. We who were sinners can now become citizens of that eternal heavenly Kingdom of God. The good news was not that the laws of the kingdom had changed, but that we could be changed to conform to that law that is good and righteous. Jesus said that He did not come to abolish the law, but to fulfill it.

Relativism, Tolerance, and Compromise

With a rewriting of history, the young people of this country have been told that the United States was established on these principles; relativism, tolerance, and compromise. Of course this is not true, but this perception has been subtly introduced over the last 100 years. What we have produced is a culture that rejects truth. They have been taught that it is wrong to claim that our government is superior to all other existing governments. They have been taught that it is wrong to say one religion is superior to another, or one is right and the other is wrong. Without a standard of right and wrong it is impossible to define the difference between good and evil. It has become so ridiculous that, in the eyes of many in this generation, the concept of a moral standard has itself become immoral.

But our nation was not founded on the basis of relativism, tolerance and compromise. This nation was founded on Biblical principles. References to God, religion, freedom, law, etc., etc., in our founding documents are all based upon the framework of a Biblical understanding. The moral values reflected by the Ten Commandments were accepted as standards. The discussions that took place were usually around what role government had in upholding those standards. Christianity was the lens through which the ideology and construction of our government and laws were formed. The ideals and ideas of freedom of religion, speech, and behavior, were constructed within this framework.

> *"I am the way, and the truth, and the life; no one comes to the Father but through Me."* (Joh 14:6 NAS95)

This is the true message of the Church and it flies in the face of this generation. But if we are going to provide anything of value to this generation we cannot compromise the truth of this message. Only adherence to the laws of the Universe can save us from certain destruction and death.

The Ten Commandments

> *"Teacher, which is the great commandment in the Law?" And He said to him, "'YOU SHALL*

> **LOVE THE LORD YOUR GOD WITH ALL YOUR HEART, AND WITH ALL YOUR SOUL, AND WITH ALL YOUR MIND.'** "This is the great and foremost commandment. "The second is like it, **'YOU SHALL LOVE YOUR NEIGHBOR AS YOURSELF.'** "On these two commandments depend the whole Law and the Prophets." (Mt 22:36-40 NAS)

If we are to truly understand God's Law then we need to view it in light of this statement of Jesus. The Law is all about love. We were created by God to love and be loved. It is in this bond of fellowship that we experience peace, contentment, fulfillment, happiness and joy, or in other words love. It is the violation of the Law of Love that has brought forth hatred, bitterness, anger, etc. etc., and death.

It is the deceptive lie, first proposed in the Garden of Eden that has raised havoc with all of creation. Today, as throughout history, people continue to be deceived into questioning the purpose and character of God and His Laws. The attack on God and His character and purpose have been relentless. The appeal to the lust of the flesh, the lust of the eye, and the pride of life has blinded people to the truth. The desire to usurp the authority of the Creator and be lord has caused people to literally shut their eyes and plug their ears to the facts contrary to the lies of Satan.

The truth is that God is good. God's commandments are for our good. The challenge of these statements first came to Eve in the Garden, but the questioning of God's goodness and the purpose of His commands continues to this day. As we consider the commandments keep in mind the understanding that Jesus revealed in answering the question of which is the greatest commandment. The fulfillment of all the commandments is to love God and love your fellow man. The Law and the Prophets are for the purpose of teaching us how to do this. We are blessed and happy when we are loved by God and our fellow man. Fulfillment of all our desires comes when simultaneously we love and are loved.

The Ten Commandments are a good place to start for building our understanding of God's Law. These fundamental, basic commands set a foundation for all the righteous laws that we could construct that would help us govern our society on every level. All of the commands that God gave to Israel were instructional to fulfill these commands. I will begin first in considering the Ten Commandments as a whole and then talking about each one individually.

These commands are the height of morality. This is ground that cannot be ceded without losing a strategic advantage in defending righteousness. The enemy knows this and this is why there has been so much effort put into removing them from the public square. Their prominence even in churches has taken a hit. Having them displayed constantly before us helps us to etch these into our memory and reflect them in our behavior. The importance of this will be understood better if we do not simply view these commands as a list of do's and don'ts. Rather we should view them as safeguards to protect us from the consequences of violating God's Law of Love.

God's Law of Love as articulated through His commands to us is not just an idea He came up with. It is actually a reflection of who He is. The consequence of violating His Law is just as real as when we violate the law of gravity. It can result in death. Only in this case it is a spiritual death of eternal consequences. When we start to see the Ten Commandments from this perspective we begin to appreciate them as the gentle reminders that are coming from a loving God.

The First Three

The first three commands reflect actions and attitudes that fulfill the first and great command that we love God with all our heart, soul, strength and mind. It is interesting that there are three commands in this section, because three is also the number of God. We who were created in God's image can also be described as body, soul, and spirit.

The Last Six Commandments

These six commandments have to do with our actions and attitudes toward our fellow man. These commandments reflect our need to love our neighbor as ourselves. Jesus said this is like the first commandment that we love God. If we follow through Scripture we will find that we cannot love God and hate our brother. When Jesus spoke about separating the sheep from the goats, judgment was based upon how people treated those in need.

"The King will answer and say to them, 'Truly I say to you, to the extent that you did it to

one of these brothers of Mine, even the least of them, you did it to Me.'" (Mt 25:40 NAS95)

Interestingly, there are six commandments that govern our relationships with each other. Six, in the Bible, is often used as the number of man.

The Commandment in Between

The fourth commandment seems to bind the first three and the last six commandments together. Jewish scholars have put it this way: "The Sabbath has kept the Jews more than the Jews have kept the Sabbath." Keeping the Sabbath honors God and could be grouped with the first three commandments. But it also plays a role in the way in which we honor each other. In addition it is also a way in which God cares for us in many personal ways. That is why I categorized it alone between the two other groups. The keeping of the Sabbath was a sign of the perpetual covenant between God and man.

The First Commandment

"You shall have no other gods before Me." (Ex 20:3 NAS95)

Now we as Christians know that there is only one God who is the creator of all that exists. That does not mean that we are ignorant of the other gods that men worship. These of course are not God. They may be spirits, demons, or Satan himself. Or they could be strictly the creation of a man's hand and/or his imagination. All of these gods are but a substitute for the God of all creation. As a substitute for God they are also substitutes for good, for God is good. Therefore, a substitute for God is evil by definition.

God is the provider of everything that is good. That is why we worship Him. Anything that exists or that we could create falls far short of the God of Abraham, Isaac, and Jacob. Our Scripture begins with the words, "In the beginning God … ". If we believe this to be true then any compromise of this commandment would defy logic. When we as Christians stand in defense or for the purpose of promoting what we believe, this is ground that cannot be ceded. Give up on this concept and we have lost every other argument.

For most of the history of our nation the overwhelming majority of its people have never had a problem acknowledging the first commandment. I suppose part of the reason comes from the fact that most of them had come from countries that embraced the Judeo-Christian morality. But what really made our national adherence to this command so powerful and long-lasting was the fact that our nation's very existence was based upon an acknowledgment of the sovereignty of the God of the Bible. Justification for rebellion from England was based upon the God-given rights of life and liberty. Freed from the dictates of kings the people of the states chose to be governed by God's Law. It was the universal acceptance of God and his Law that became the unifying feature that identified us as a nation. And God blessed this nation in as much as they acknowledged His sovereignty. And we prospered as no other nation on earth.

The results caught the attention of the world. The blessing of God rested upon this people who were governed according to the wisdom that had come from above. God was honored in the home and in the public square. The resulting civility became a standard even for those who did not embrace God's Word. Those who came from other lands and cultures that had embraced other gods were impacted as they came to these shores. Many were won over to the worship of the God of the Bible because of the way faith was lived out in the lives of the believers.

Of course, this country was not without its challenges, and they came from all sides. But our system survived because when times got tough people realized that they needed to again commit themselves to the principles that had brought them blessings from God. And when as a nation the people turned toward God He met us with healing and blessing.

For almost 400 years, from the Pilgrims until the year 2000, the people of this land and the nation that was birthed here honored the first commandment. It may be argued that by the year 2000 many that honored the God of the Bible did so in word only and not in deed. Then in the year 2000, Congress for the first time, opened their session by having a Hindu offer the opening prayer. As far as I know this was the first official action of our government to call on another god for blessings. The implications were staggering, a betrayal of our faith and heritage, and an indication of our future direction. By the year 2008 President Obama declared that we are no longer a Christian nation. Since that time many of those in governmental positions have shown more respect to the god of Islam than to the

Christian God. For many it has become politically correct to show equal respect to all religions and their gods.

This is ground that we as Christians must not cede. The God of all creation will not settle for equal standing with the gods of man's creation. Nor will He share His supreme status with Satan or any of the angels. We dare not be on the wrong side of this dispute.

The defense of our stance on this commandment is as simple as one, two, three. If we believe that God has created all that exists, then He has no equal. No logic in the world would put any part of His creation before Him in our respect, acknowledgement, and worship. Even more ridiculous would be worship of a god of our imagination or the creation of our hands. The calls to respect religious diversity fly in the face of reality. If the Christian God is the creator of all things then He alone is worthy of worship and prayer. But if multiple gods are worthy of respect, then what is the point? Will we serve gods that are merely the creation of man's imagination?

There are well-meaning people that argue that when we show respect, we are just showing respect for those who believe in these gods and not actually worshiping their gods. What they fail to consider is the blatant disrespect they are giving to the one and only Creator.

The Second Commandment

"You shall not make for yourself an idol, or any likeness of what is in heaven above or on the

> *earth beneath or in the water under the earth.*
> *"You shall not worship them or serve them; for I,*
> *the LORD your God, am a jealous God, visiting*
> *the iniquity of the fathers on the children, on*
> *the third and the fourth generations of those*
> *who hate Me, but showing lovingkindness to*
> *thousands, to those who love Me and keep My*
> *commandments."* (Ex 20:4-6 NAS95)

An image, an idol, or a likeness of anything never is fully adequate in its depiction of the real thing. To be sure, modern technology has come a long way and could add to the imagery, action, and sound. But it would still be lacking in portraying the real thing. Even we as humans are far more than the physical bodies in which we live.

Because we were created in the image and likeness of God, the true essence of who we are is largely invisible and best known through personal relationships. The appearance of our physical body can be misleading if taken as a reflection of our essence or who we really are. This concept was brought out in that classic film "The Hunchback of Notre Dame". A kind and gentle person was living in a gross deformed body of the Hunchback, whereas a vile self-centered evil man was living in a dignified- appearing body of a churchman. Physical appearances can be deceptive. This is especially true when we consider that individual interpretations of what the physical appearance represents (good or evil) is often based on the individual's own experience, which can vary dramatically person to person.

Is it any surprise then that God does not want us to represent Him with physical imagery?

> **"God is spirit, and those who worship Him must worship in spirit and truth."** (Joh 4:24 NAS)

God knows us by who we are. He wants us to know Him by who He is. We learn about Him through His creation, His Word (both written and revealed in the flesh), and His Spirit. Basic understanding of who He is helps us to understand how little we can impress Him with our physical gifts. Just a simple study of the names God uses to describe Himself to us surpasses any imagery we could create of Him. Simply put, any imagery would give a false impression of God.

God knows, and history reveals, how easily people can be distracted and inclined to worship things. Religions are full of sacred idols, items, practices, and places. All these are diversions for that which is real and holy. Any argument that any of these things can contribute to true worship is swallowed up in the reality of the history of these inconsequential items. These things themselves become the focus of worship, a focus that belongs only to God. Men market in these items, they fight over them, and they kill because of them. Only God is worthy of our worship. His mercy and loving-kindness are extended to those who follow His commands. We need to stand our ground on this important issue.

> **"And even if our gospel is veiled, it is veiled to those who are perishing, in whose case the god of this world has blinded the minds of the**

*unbelieving so that they might not see the light
of the gospel of the glory of Christ, who is the
image of God."* (2Co 4:3-4 NAS95)

The god of this world would like for us to remain blinded by images, either physical or imagined, that can be manipulated for his benefit. But God would have us see His image that was revealed in the personage of Jesus Christ. God has revealed Himself so that we may truly worship Him in spirit and in truth. Christ left no physical picture or image of himself, rather he left us with his words and actions, revealing His very essence. The closest to a physical depiction of God we have is seen in mankind themselves, who were created in the image and likeness of God. Of a truth that image has been marred by sin, but yet there remains a semblance of the variety, grace, and beauty that must reside in God Himself, the Creator of us all.

God alone is worthy of worship because of who He is. Not only is He the Creator of all things eternal and omnipotent, but He is just and kind and has offered us a place with Him forever.

The Third Commandment

*"You shall not take the name of the LORD your
God in vain, for the LORD will not leave him
unpunished who takes His name in vain."* (Ex 20:7 NAS95)

I grew up at a time and place where this commandment was taken very seriously. As a society the attitude toward this commandment has changed dramatically in my lifetime. Respectfully refraining from using the Lord's name in vain around people of faith or even in the general public was the norm a few years ago. Today there seems to be a blatant disregard for this commandment. Probably there is a large segment of our society that is not even aware of what this commandment says.

Generally speaking the language of our present culture is cruder, ruder, and less respectful all around than it was 50 years ago. Degrading language concerning private bodily functions have become common spontaneous expressions. People banter these expressions mindlessly with seemingly no regard for their obscene literal meaning. Language, of course, is just one indicator of the direction a society is moving in. But the context of the expressions of God's name becomes a clear indicator of the respect or disrespect people have for the personage represented by the name.

You would have to be blind and deaf to not notice that the attitudes of our culture in general have influenced those who claim to be followers of Christ, and the broader population that consider themselves to be Christian. As previously discussed, our American culture began under the influence of Christianity and as such was built upon the moral foundation of Christian doctrine. Presently the flow of influence is in the opposite direction. Anti-Christian sentiment rules the direction of our country and is affecting the moral perspective even in many churches. Often the changes that happen in churches are subtle and escape people's notice. But when we come back to God's Word and consider His commandments we are made keenly aware of the drift that has taken place and how far we have gone.

The most common way in which this commandment was followed by Christians was in our language or our usage of God's name. Possibly the warning included in the commandment explains why it was taken so seriously. Again, I want to remind you that 100 years ago we lived in a much more respectful society. Much more respect was given to God and to those created in His image. During that time people created names that are similar to God's name, but spelled different. I guess the purpose of this was so they would still be able to shout out God's name without experiencing the full displeasure of a Christian society. We call those words slang and they include expressions such as, gosh, golly, and gees.

In the home I grew up in the slang terms were as bad as saying the real thing. But by the time I grew up some of these words were becoming common language even among Christians. At present date even preachers use some of these slang words in their discourses from the pulpit. Many do not even know that these words are slang for names of God. I know this, because I have challenged people to look up their meanings in the dictionary.

So, what is in a name, and why is it so important to God? The answer should be obvious. A name represents who you are. In the Old Testament God used several expressive names for Himself to reveal His character to us. Most revealing was the name He gave to Moses. The children of Israel had been living for 400 years amongst a people who worshiped many gods. So God told Moses, to tell them that "I Am" sent him. This descriptive name for God set Him apart from all of the gods of the

Egyptians. This name distinguished Him as the one and only uncreated being.

Using a name inaccurately falsely portrays a person as something that they are not. To use God's name in a way that misrepresents Him is as wrong as presenting Him as a dog or a tree. It is wrong to slander a person in such a way as to destroy their reputation. How much worse it is to misrepresent God, the Creator of all things, and slander the very source of good. It is foolish for the ignorant to try to bring God down to our level. But those who have even had a glimpse of the goodness and glory of God should instinctively know better.

What does it mean to take God's name in vain? Those who have a better understanding of the Hebrew language than I do tell us that what the commandment is really saying is: You shall not carry the Lord's name in vain. There is a subtle difference between the words "take" and "carry". The emphasis I grew up with was that you do not use the name of the Lord in an inappropriate manner. Certainly this would be a way to carry the Lord's name in vain. To use the Lord's name as a swear word or in such a way that would put the blame on Him for something that was the result of evil is certainly carrying His name in vain. But I believe that there is a broader meaning also that would include those who carry His name as a banner for their causes, and this is also included in this commandment and is a serious violation of the commandment.

When kings, rulers, or politicians have inspired people to take up a cause under the banner of Our Lord's Name, it is a blatant violation of this commandment. To brand human endeavors, no matter how noble we think they are, with God's name is a misrepresentation of God and His purposes. This is not to say that we cannot band together under the banner of God's Name. But if we do we need to be careful that we are not misrepresenting God in the process. The only way to do that is to move in accordance to the Word of God.

Jesus came bearing, or carrying, the Name of God. In all that He did and said He represented His Father in heaven. We also can do the works of our Father in heaven. We can and should also declare His Word to our generation. But we need to be careful not to put God's name on the works and ambitions of men.

If we call ourselves Christians, then we bear the name of Christ. Think about it. People in our society used to be more aware of the honor or dishonor that we can bring to our family name. How much more we should be aware of the honor or dishonor we bring to Christ's name if we bear it by calling ourselves Christians.

As Christians we cannot cede the moral high ground and compromise this commandment. Societies have laws intended to protect people from falsely slandering men's names and reputations. Heaven also has laws that preserve truth. God is the arbitrator and judge in these matters and those who violate this command will not go unpunished. If we care about people and love like God loves we will not hide this commandment from their understanding. Our obligation as Christians is to fulfill this commandment in both word and deed. It is our duty to live it as a testimony of our respect for the love of God and teach other to do so likewise.

The Fourth Commandment

*"Remember the sabbath day, to keep it holy.
"Six days you shall labor and do all your work,
but the seventh day is a sabbath of the LORD
your God; in it you shall not do any work, you
or your son or your daughter, your male or your
female servant or your cattle or your sojourner
who stays with you. "For in six days the LORD
made the heavens and the earth, the sea and
all that is in them, and rested on the seventh
day; therefore the LORD blessed the sabbath
day and made it holy."* (Ex 20:8-11 NAS95)

Remember the Sabbath, to keep it holy.

In my previous generalization of the Ten Commandments
I pointed out that keeping the first three commandments
demonstrates our love, honor, and respect for God. The last
six commandments demonstrate our love, honor and respect
for our fellow human beings that were created in the image
of God. The fourth commandment seems to bring us together
with God in many ways. Every seventh day was to be set apart
(sanctified), hallowed as a day when we cease our labor. It is
a day for communion, fellowship, reflection, and worship. It is
a day in which we are to put aside our individual pursuits and
ambitions, cease from our labors, and rest.

The seven-day week is a unique element of our calendars. The
day, month, and year, are all based upon the timing established
by our solar system. But the seven-day week was established

by God as He created our world and all that is herein. It is more than just an arbitrary number of days to keep track of time, it actually seems like our internal clock was established on a seven-day cycle. When we ignore this signature of God that He patterned at creation, we soon suffer the consequences. Loss of productivity, fatigue, irritability, and depression are just some of the symptoms. In a culture of greed and ambition there is a push for a 24/7 culture, often our natural functions rebel.

The seventh day provides a time to reboot. Our lives get cluttered and fragmented, and that clutter gets mixed with that which is good and necessary. A pause every seventh day allows us time to evaluate everything and reboot, start over, and begin each week refreshed and focused. Our pause is not arbitrary, but provides a gentle reminder of who we are and where we came from. "Remember the Sabbath and keep it holy". Regardless of which day you consider the Sabbath (I won't get into that discussion here) it is essential that we go back to the former practice of setting this day aside to honor God.

> *"More than the Jewish People have kept the Sabbath, the Sabbath has kept the Jews."*
> *— Ahad Ha'am*

A book could be written in support of keeping the Sabbath and the valuable benefits that would result from just this one practice. But the most important reason for keeping God's Sabbaths is found in the narrative in Exodus as God was instituting the keeping of the Sabbath with the Hebrew people He had just delivered from bondage. God had separated these people from the world to be a nation, a people in which he would reveal

Himself to the world. The keeping of the Sabbaths was to be a sign, a perpetual sign, of His covenant with them.

> *"'So the sons of Israel shall observe the sabbath, to celebrate the sabbath throughout their generations as a perpetual covenant.' "It is a sign between Me and the sons of Israel forever; for in six days the LORD made heaven and earth, but on the seventh day He ceased [from labor,] and was refreshed."* (Ex 31:16-17 NAS95)

When Christ came He did not come to abolish the law, but to fulfill it. Jesus kept the Sabbath and so did His followers. Our observance of the Sabbath is still intended to be a sign between God and those who are separated unto Him. It is an outward sign that the entire world can see. It is a signature of the Creator on His created World. When it is observed it brings great blessings to the observers. All of creation was intended to pause and take a breath and be refreshed every seventh day. This is the design and signature of the creator and becomes a sign of covenant with those who choose to comply.

I will not go into the science of the health and mental benefits that would be gleaned from observance of a seventh day set aside for rest and refreshing. These benefits are here for all who simply structure their lives after this pattern. But for the Christian who maintains this day for the spiritual benefits, this practice is of great spiritual value, far exceeding its physical benefits.

I believe there is a lot of truth in Ahad Ha'am's statement about the Sabbath's role in preserving the Jewish people. I also believe it is true concerning the preservation of Christianity. Today in our Western societies we have experienced a tremendous decline in the numbers of those who practice Biblical Christianity as well as Judaism. A great deal of this decline can be attributed to the failure to simply obey this one commandment to "Remember the Sabbath to keep it holy". I am not saying that decline in Biblical Christianity has not in turn affected how many people keep the Sabbath. What I am saying is that neglecting the keeping of the Sabbath happened first and has had the greatest impact.

Historically the Church, and people in general seem to have a tendency to stray from the principles of truth and goodness that provide the basis for love and peace. The Ten Commandments preserve the Godly principles that provide a fundamental structure for culture. If this structure remains intact when people stray, then the return to godly living is a matter of repentance and revival. But when that structure is broken down a rebirth is required and much harder to accomplish. That is why the Church in America has been able to rebound so many times in our short history, because the fundamental structure established by the Ten Commandments was not discarded. That is also why in America, Christianity seems to be in a death spiral today, because by and large that structure that was rooted in our society has been discarded. That structure of law and order that is part of the character of God is in the process of even being discarded by those who still claim to be Christian.

This commandment to honor the Sabbath and keep it holy seems to have fallen first and has been rationalized as not that important. Yet the effect of neglecting to keep the Sabbath has proven otherwise. This is the one commandment that patterns our lives to ensure our personal and corporate fellowship with God. This was the sign of our covenant with God to separate ourselves from the World and unto Him. This was our opportunity to fulfill our obligation to our children to teach them the ways of God and our reliance on Him. This was a sign that we had truly put God first in our lives.

When we fail this commandment, then it fails us. Jesus so clearly stated that this commandment was made for us. It is fulfilled to our advantage and our good, and when that happens it is for the glory of God. Even in the Church the commandments are beginning to fall, one by one, and I believe it began right here with neglect to remember the Sabbath and keep it holy.

I was privileged to have been born in a conservative Christian family in small American town. But subtly and gradually even here the corruption of this nation is manifest all around us. Having been born in the early 1950's I have lived long enough to have observed the dramatic changes taking place in the moral climate of this nation. I can still remember the Easter sunrise services that took place at the high school football field, sponsored by the combined efforts of the various churches in town. When I graduated from high school we still had baccalaureate services in which all the students gathered to be encouraged and blessed by those who prayed in Jesus' name for His blessing upon us. How our country has changed in a few short years.

The commandments fall because of subtle compromises that may not have seemed important at the time. There have been a lot of things that eroded the customs of our culture that once honored Sunday as a Sabbath to the Lord. I will offer one example that impacted my area. Sunday was a day in which most stores were closed, except service stations and restaurants. Then gradually malls were introduced. With the malls came seven-day retail. All sorts of businesses were in the mall and the pressure was on to remain open seven days a week. Convenience soon broke down the resolve of many of those who used to honor the Sabbath as a day to cease their labor. It was not long before Sunday became just another day to do business. The ripple effect was tremendous from just the contribution of this one thing. Why did it have such an effect? It was effective simply because of people's lack of resolve to carefully follow God's Law. If enough people had continued to honor the Sabbath, then the mall would have closed its doors on Sunday.

Again God's people have ceded the high ground on this issue. This command came from the loving concern of our Father in Heaven. It is backed by moral conviction, our need for rest, refreshing, contemplation, acknowledgement of creation and the Creator, worship, family and the Law of Love. There is no good reason for us not to follow this commandment, the world's arguments fall flat in light of history and reason.

I have spent a considerable amount of time on this one commandment. I guess that is because I have come to see it as somewhat of a sentinel commandment. Following this commandment provided the means to preserve our awareness of the Law of God and its importance. As adherence to this commandment waned the subtle compromise of the other commandments began to erode one by one. As I have already mentioned, I believe this commandment alone has had a tremendous influence in preserving Christianity in a pagan world. I could go on and on about the importance of this commandment that is rooted in the creation of the World. Yet I have watched in my lifetime how the American Churches have allowed it to fade to obscurity without scarcely a whimper.

The lack of defense of this one commandment has wracked havoc on the churches. What has been proven to be true is that simply attending church was not enough. Keeping the Sabbath holy was about sanctifying the whole day. This commandment like all of the rest of them was intended to keep us safe and secure. Compromise of this commandment compromises our safety and security, leaving the church and its people vulnerable to attack.

One other thing that I believe that is usually overlooked is the effect that adherence to this commandment has had on the world around us. I think keeping the Sabbath has had a greater affect on the world than our keeping of any of the other commandments. Keeping the Sabbath has impacted the entire world, testifying of the God of Creation. No other commandment has had as far reaching and as powerful effect as this one commandment when it was adhered to. It is no wonder that this is where the attack of the enemy has come and been most successful. Downgrading this commandment undermined the power to keep the church pure and its power to impact the culture.

The Fifth Commandment

"Honor your father and your mother, that your days may be prolonged in the land which the LORD your God gives you." (Ex 20:12 NAS95)

God is a God of Love. I remind you about this because in essence all the commandments of based upon God's love for us and through us. His relationship to mankind is based upon this foundational fact. For anyone intent upon doing what is good and right, this is where they have to start. Of course, I am not talking about emotional feelings of ecstasy that come with anticipation of having our desires satisfied. This is the world's concept of love. The love I am talking about is that genuine concern for someone else's well being. In return we all enjoy being loved. The ideal relationship is one in which both parties put the well-being of the other first and foremost in their actions. And in return they both enjoy the affections shown to them.

"We love, because He first loved us."
(1Jo 4:19 NAS95)

God first initiated love toward us. We in turn are to be the initiators in our relationships with others. None of the commandments of God are contingent upon the actions of others. If they were contingent upon someone else's actions then there would be no hope. Think about it.

There is no better place to begin teaching about human relationships than with our first human relationship. It is on this fundamental level that God intended to build all our future relationships. Love should first start at home. Except in those cases where evil has so overtaken an individual that all vestiges of the original image and likeness of God have been erased, a mother's love comes naturally with the arrival of her child. Likewise, especially when the child is the product of a committed relationship, the father has a natural affection toward his child. This commandment is a reminder to honor this God given-gift of love that comes through our parents.

I want to emphasize that the commands of God are not contingent upon the action of anyone else. Parents are sometimes not as good or as loving as they should be. Some parents are actually bad parents who have allowed selfish desires to overcome their natural God-given inclinations. On both sides of this relationship there exists a natural inclination toward selfishness that has come to us through our bondage to sin and rebellion. God-given desires, and sin-induced desires, are at war, hence the need for this command.

A father and mother is a couple who have had the privilege of introducing a new life into the world. This is in the plan of God and as parents a mother and father hold a privileged and responsible position. God has honored them with this position and requires their children to honor their position also. And of course, by honoring them we also honor God the giver of life and love. As with all of the commandments, following the commandment is intended to be an act of love toward God and those who were created in the image and likeness of God.

"Children, obey your parents in the Lord, for this is right. HONOR YOUR FATHER AND MOTHER

(which is the first commandment with a promise), SO THAT IT MAY BE WELL WITH YOU, AND THAT YOU MAY LIVE LONG ON THE EARTH."
(Eph 6:1-3 NAS95)

Parents are responsible for the caring of their children physically, mentally, and spiritually. To fulfill their responsibility God has granted them authority over their children. When we are children the fulfillment of this commandment simply is for us to live in obedience under our parent's authority. Of course, this does not give parents the right to misuse and abuse their children for they are required to live under the authority of their father in heaven. God is a God of order.

Relationships with parents and the way in which they are honored changes as children grow, mature, and become parents themselves. In some ways it is also true concerning our relationship with our Father in heaven. Jesus quotes a passage from Genesis that says: *"Therefore shall a man leave his father and his mother, and shall cleave unto his wife: and they shall be one flesh."* (Ge 2:24 AV) Obviously the relationship changes, but the commandment is still in effect.

Children honor their parents by submitting to their authority in the home in which they live and showing proper respect. In this setting the parents provide for the necessities of the child. But Jesus chided the Pharisees because of their failing in this command when they neglected to provide necessities for their aging parents. Furthermore, their gifts to God did not exempt them from fulfilling their responsibility to honor their father and mother.

> *"He was also saying to them, "You are experts
> at setting aside the commandment of God in
> order to keep your tradition. "For Moses said,
> 'HONOR YOUR FATHER AND YOUR MOTHER';
> and, 'HE WHO SPEAKS EVIL OF FATHER OR
> MOTHER, IS TO BE PUT TO DEATH'; but you say,
> 'If a man says to [his] father or [his] mother,
> whatever I have that would help you is Corban
> (that is to say, given [to God),'] you no longer
> permit him to do anything for [his] father or
> [his] mother; [thus] invalidating the word of
> God by your tradition which you have handed
> down; and you do many things such as that.""*
> (Mr 7:9-13 NAS95)

Relationships are important to God, not only with Him but with people, starting right here with our father and mother. Failure to keep them brings a curse on us, but keeping them brings the blessing of God. Paul points to the blessing and states that this is the first commandment with promise: "... **SO THAT IT MAY BE WELL WITH YOU, AND THAT YOU MAY LIVE LONG ON THE EARTH.**" (Eph 6:1-3 NAS95)

A book could be written revealing the realities that have come about simply because of the neglect of this one commandment. The disruption of peace and contentment begins in the home and spreads to the world around us. Today the disruption of parental authority is celebrated as our society unravels around us. Again, time and history have proven that those who maintain the commandments of God to be good and profitable hold the high ground on parental authority and honor.

The Sixth Commandment

"You shall not murder." (Ex 20:13 NAS95)

Some things seem so clear and obvious that a person would think further explanation was not necessary. But because we have a tendency to rationalize and excuse bad behavior it is necessary to spell out simple principles in various ways to leave no doubt as to proper behavior. Simply put, we do not have the authority to take another humans life. Further Biblical explanation and commandments make it very clear that we are to value human's life because we were created in the likeness and image of God.

This commandment, like all the rest of them, did not originate when God wrote it on stone and handed it to Moses. Moses presented the Hebrews with commandments from which mankind had already strayed so far from. The Law of God that forbade the taking of human life was present from the very beginning. This principle suffered its first violation when Cain killed Abel. God created man in his own image and likeness. Man was the crown of God's creation and it is reasonable to conclude that the created world in which we live, the earth and its heavens were made for man. God not only gave man dominion over all the earth, but He also gave man the ability and charge to reproduce and have sons and daughters. Of all creation, man alone was created with an eternal soul, life that was drawn from the breath of God.

> *"Whoever sheds man's blood, By man his blood shall be shed, For in the image of God He made man."* (Ge 9:6 NAS95)

A fundamental understanding of the basics of creation gives us the understanding of the sacredness of human life. God, the creator, the giver of life, alone has the right to take life. It is God's judgment and His alone that determines the requirement of a man's life to be taken from him. Since Cain people have come up with every reason imaginable to justify the taking of another life. In so doing they incur the wrath of God and bring sentence down upon themselves.

As far as we know the 20th century was the bloodiest in history with millions of casualties. This century may be even worse, if God allows us to continue. Here in America, where the cultural influence of Christianity has prevailed until this century, human life has become subjective. Christianity produced a culture that revered each individual life. The United States was founded on the principle of life as a right granted by God Himself. But now, as this nation turns from God and rejects His precepts, life itself has become subjective. Since 1973 it has become lawful in this nation to kill the unborn, snuff out a person's life before they see the light of day. More than 50 million have been brutally murdered in this way. This culture of death has spread across the globe. Next we are beginning to push the premature killing of those who are sick and elderly.

As we as a nation drift further from the precepts of God and the concept that all men are created equal, and thus are all held to the same standard, we experience a breakdown in civility.

It was the acknowledgment of God that produced our unity, the acknowledgment of a higher authority. As that authority is rejected we continue to become more divided. Rhetoric that was once only used by the criminal element has now entered mainstream. For many, some people's lives matter more than others. It is becoming so heated that some are suggesting murders would be justified, simply for a difference of opinion.

> *"For You formed my inward parts; You wove me in my mother's womb. I will give thanks to You, for I am fearfully and wonderfully made; Wonderful are Your works, And my soul knows it very well. My frame was not hidden from You, When I was made in secret, [And] skillfully wrought in the depths of the earth; Your eyes have seen my unformed substance; And in Your book were all written The days that were ordained [for me,] When as yet there was not one of them."* (Ps 139:13-16 NAS95)

Whether we are talking about abortion, euthanasia, or simply murder, we who have put our trust in God's Word and His commandments have always held the high ground. Now, of all times in history, we need to hold fast to that high ground. Modern science has uncovered the knowledge that from the moment of conception every detail of our unformed bodies was determined. Knowing this we have full understanding of when the choice to create life was in our hands. After conception the determined life forms without any input from us and is a separate person. Is this new life subject to our whims and desires, to be disposed of at will? Or is this a sacred trust we have been given to protect and nourish this little one as God forms this person according to the predetermined plan? Accepting the sacred trust is the moral high ground.

The Seventh Commandment

"You shall not commit adultery." (Ex 20:14 NAS95)

The commandments of God are about doing the right thing. Those that rebel against these commandments still want to be treated with respect. They usually do not have any objection to restrictions placed on others not to murder them, or in this case having sex with their wife or husband. So they propose that following these rules should be arbitrary. For them right and wrong is relative to the situation and circumstances. Of course, to make this case we have to link those circumstances to one person as being the center and everyone else's opinion taking a different relative value.

I admit that violation of the simple commands of God becomes relative to the circumstances and situations. When a person puts themselves above the commandment there can be relatively few or relatively many people that are adversely affected. But someone or ones will suffer if the commandments are violated. It is the mutual respect and value of each person that the commandments are intended to teach us to honor.

This commandment is based upon the fundamental relationship between man and woman that God established in the very beginning.

"And He answered and said, "Have you not read that He who created [them] from the beginning MADE THEM MALE AND FEMALE, and said, 'FOR THIS REASON A MAN SHALL LEAVE HIS FATHER AND MOTHER AND BE JOINED TO HIS WIFE, AND THE TWO SHALL BECOME ONE FLESH'? "So they are no longer two, but one flesh. What therefore God has joined together, let no man separate." (Mt 19:4-6 NAS95)

Marriage vows were created to reflect these established facts. God's plan for mankind is based in this basic established relationship between a man and a woman. The commitment of those in this relationship is that the two become one. The consummation of this relationship produces children who share the two in their one. This is a sacred relationship, the violation of which adversely affects all of those involved. Two family structures are violated by adultery that can be disruptive for generations.

Rationalization of the breaking of this commandment has to center on the individual. For the effects to our society as a whole cannot be hidden. The temporary feelings of one or two individuals are allowed to trump the poverty, rejection, abandonment, and multiple other effects on those around them. Many have argued that because of human resilience and because we can develop new relationships, that we will be able to recover and it will be all right in the end. Reality testifies otherwise. Scars remain as our society continues to spiral downward.

If we are talking about morals, right and wrong that includes everyone, then upholding this commandment is the moral high ground.

The Eighth Commandment

"You shall not steal." (Ex 20:15 NAS95)

I think that everyone would agree that they do not want anyone to steal from them. But it is amazing how many people justify stealing from someone else. Probably the easiest way to justify stealing is to depersonalize it. If people steal from the government, a corporation, or a store, they rationalize that it does not affect real people. The reality is that if we take something that does not belong to us then some person or people pay for what we have taken.

The fundamental principles presented in the commandments cannot be violated without having destructive consequences. Even in those cases where the violation of these fundamentals was motivated by compassion, or a desire to achieve justice or equality, the end product is lawlessness. The end does not justify the means. You cannot achieve righteousness through lawlessness. The commandments reflect righteousness. You cannot ever find a shortcut to the end of a straight line.

As we as a nation drifted from the principle of laws for the protection of the individual, we migrated to a creation of laws that give certain segments of society an advantage. It does not take a rocket scientist to figure out that this creates an atmosphere of competition in which people try to use law to their personal advantage. Theft is often rationalized to create equality, but in the end righteousness and justice are lost. We have now created possibly one to two million laws in our quest to maintain order, simply because we have compromised simple principles such as: "You shall not steal".

In essence people have devised "legal" means to steal other people's stuff. Without the restraints of these simple Ten Commandments people have devised hundreds of ways to steal what belongs to another person. The multitude of ambiguous and conflicting laws have opened the doors for our courts to be a means to extract wealth and redistribute it through lawsuits and other legal wrangling. Our tax system has become a means of an unrighteous manipulation of wealth. The lack of morals and the influences of drugs and alcohol have created an escalation of blatant theft and lawlessness. These things alone will eventually destroy a society. But if all this was not enough we now have unrestrained borrowing.

Deficit spending with no intention to repay the debt is theft. For a time there is an illusion of prosperity. For a while you can feel good about all the good things you can accomplish with the borrowed money. But in the end when your debt has exceeded your collateral, then your house of cards will collapse. As our country continues to drift from its Christian roots the checks and balances intended to keep us safe also erode.

"Our Constitution was made only for a moral and religious people. It is wholly inadequate to the government of any other." *John Adams*

When we as a people are no longer restrained by the laws of God, theft then becomes commonplace. Our outrage is only expressed when we feel that we personally have been violated. The huge debt our country is accruing will not be paid by those who are using this money to pursue their ends. This is theft from our grandchildren and great-grandchildren. In essence, it is selling them into slavery.

When I was in the army my friend and I bought a small refrigerator for our sodas in the barracks. One day upon returning, we confronted one of our friends drinking one of our sodas from our fridge. When asked how he could blatantly steal from us, he explained that he had not stolen from us. Rather he was given the soda from others who had stolen from our fridge.

This simple incident illustrates what is happening on a much larger scale. People are being bribed with stolen goods to cause them to ignore the travesty that is taking place right in front of them. One of the side effects of this is the creation of generations of people who believe they are entitled to this borrowed money. They have received so much without any effort on their part that they have lost touch with reality. The truth is that someone has to pay and we are beginning to pay in big ways.

So how did we get to this point where 40% of our Federal expenditures come from borrowed money? We ended up here because we ceded the high moral ground that it is wrong to steal. It is wrong to borrow money you do not intend to pay back. What we have allowed was for the argument to take place on the level of those who are benefiting from theft. At that level it is easy to rationalize and focus on the benefits of lawless behavior. But God said: "You shall not steal".

The Ninth Commandment

"You shall not bear false witness against your neighbor." (Ex 20:16 NAS95)

We live in a culture that is rapidly becoming secular. The secular culture rejects the Ten Commandments because they come from the Bible. They claim that in rejecting the concept of a transcendent being and the spiritual realm they are able to rely on facts and reason. Arguing as they do leads them to a realm of circular reasoning and constant contradictions. To lower ourselves to their level of reasoning results in futile bantering that never culminates in truth. Truth, they have been taught, is relative. The truth is that ignoring absolutes is dangerous.

As I have pointed out, these commandments are for the purpose of teaching and guiding us to love our fellow human beings. Bearing false witness is deception. Regardless of the motivation, false witness is telling or living a lie, or both. Regardless of the motivation, false testimony's final result will be harmful.

"and you will know the truth, and the truth will make you free." (Joh 8:32 NAS95)

"Jesus *said to him, "I am the way, and the truth, and the life; no one comes to the Father but through Me." (Joh 14:6 NAS95)

"Sanctify them in the truth; Your word is truth."
(Joh 17:17 NAS95)

Truth and reality are in essence the same thing. Why then is it even necessary to defend the rightness of a command to tell the truth. The traditions in our culture are reflected in the courtrooms where false testimony is outlawed with penalties for violating this law. We used to raise our children emphasizing the importance of telling the truth. As time has gone on, gradually the rationalization of exceptions has undermined the importance and value of living and speaking the truth.

This digression of the valuation of truth has brought our society to a dangerous low. The blurring of the line between truth and fantasy seems to have affected every area of our culture. Confusion and delusion have somehow become the norm. Technology has contributed to our confusion by allowing people to view everything in the cyber world, a world that can be manipulated to make anything seem real. As people spend large portions of their lives in this make-believe world they struggle to face the real world where the laws of God and nature unwaveringly exist.

A list of the excuses, and explaining the rational for distorting the truth, would fill a book. An analysis of these excuses would reveal that distortions of the truth always favor a person or persons at the expense of others. In the end, God's judgment of liars is that they will not inherit eternal life in the presence of our Lord and Savior.

"Do you solemnly swear that you will tell the truth, the whole truth, and nothing but the truth, so help you God?"

Our common oath given in a court of law expresses an understanding of what bearing false testimony really is. First, telling the truth. Secondly, telling the whole truth, because it is only the whole truth that gives an accurate picture of any situation. Thirdly, nothing but the truth, because anything added that is not accurate contaminates the truth of the testimony.

As our country has neglected the commandments of our Lord, the focus in the courtroom has shifted from truth, righteousness, and justice, to achieving victory. With the shifting of the goal from judgment to victory the whole process becomes perverted. Both sides in this drama have the tendency to suppress elements of the whole truth through courtroom manipulation. There is also the tendency to try to introduce elements that are not entirely true or accurate.

The rejection of this simple commandment that you do not give false testimony results in a society that does not have mutual respect one for another. Lying and deception are commonplace throughout every aspect of our society. No one likes to be lied to or deceived. So the battles rage throughout our society as people argue their individual cases, not willing to give up their own exception. As a society we simply cannot make any headway toward achieving righteousness and justice as long as we argue our cases from a lower level. It is only from the high ground of God's commandment of *"You shall not bear false testimony"*, that we can achieve justice.

God has ordained that governments be established on earth to carry out the judgment of God. It is in the controlled atmosphere of a courtroom that this is possible. As we can see when the concept of truth is compromised, then judgments even in the courtroom get tainted. Even more evident as we leave the courtroom and enter the public square true justice becomes elusive without truth. Our culture has rejected God and expelled His Law from the public square. In our increasingly lawless land false testimony is abundant. Starting with gossip magazines and finally becoming the norm in the mainline press, false news and fake news are filled with false testimony. As this climate persists people become enraged and judgment is often carried out in the public square.

Laying aside the foundational precepts upon which our nation was founded, people are losing their positions, jobs, and reputations without the benefit of a trial or any of the benefits intended by our legal system. Public opinion stirred up by false testimony is stripping people of their dignity, livelihood, and sometimes even their life.

The bottom line is that people have lost their fear of God. Without the truth, the whole truth, and nothing but the truth, justice is lost. I have heard mobs chanting, "NO JUSTICE, NO PEACE", but it is their rejection of order and truth that precludes justice and insures that there will be no peace. They march for victory, not justice, for if they were concerned with justice they would seek truth. Perjury is a serious offence in God's Book.

The Tenth Commandment

> *"You shall not covet your neighbor's house;*
> *you shall not covet your neighbor's wife or his*
> *male servant or his female servant or his ox*
> *or his donkey or anything that belongs to your*
> *neighbor."* (Ex 20:17 NAS95)

Is this the mother of all the commandments? Is not this where most of our problems with the commandments begin? Is not coveting or desiring something that belongs to someone else often the root cause for violating the other commandments? Why does a person murder, steal, lie, or commit adultery? Usually it begins with a desire for something that is not theirs. That desire can be for a thing, but can also be jealous envy for a position or approval that someone else has received. The point is that the sin of coveting usually leads to other sins.

Before a person sins he is usually confronted with a temptation. In the Book of James he points to the source of that temptation, which is lust or desire.

> *"But each one is tempted when he is carried*
> *away and enticed by his own lust. Then when*
> *lust has conceived, it gives birth to sin; and*
> *when sin is accomplished, it brings forth death."*
> (Jas 1:14-15 NAS)

Later James names the same source for wars and fighting among them.

> *"What is the source of quarrels and conflicts among you? Is not the source your pleasures that wage war in your members? You lust and do not have; so you commit murder. And you are envious and cannot obtain; so you fight and quarrel. You do not have because you do not ask. You ask and do not receive, because you ask with wrong motives, so that you may spend it on your pleasures."* (Jas 4:1-3 NAS)

Lusts or desires in themselves can be good or bad. It is not wrong to desire a wife. But it is wrong to wish to fulfill that desire by depriving another man of his wife. The same is true for anything that belongs to someone else. God-given desires are to be fulfilled from a God-given source. James points us to the source for the fulfillment of our desires, God. You may not have what you desire because you are trying to get it from the wrong place. You do not have because you did not ask. And what you did, ask for you asked for the wrong reasons.

God has provided for us everything that we would need and many pleasures besides. When we try to bypass the path that God has provided to receive our desires, we undermine his plan and purpose for us.

> *"Do not be deceived, my beloved brethren. Every good thing bestowed and every perfect gift is from above, coming down from the Father of lights, with whom there is no variation, or shifting shadow."* (Jas 1:16-17 NAS)

If we look back to the first sin we can see that Eve was deceived when Satan created in her a desire for what was not hers to partake of. Eve saw that the tree was good for food, pleasing to the eyes, and desirable to make one wise; she partook and ate of the fruit.

Today in the United States we live in probably the most affluent and charitable country that has ever existed on earth. Even though in my lifetime we have reached our pinnacle and are in steady decline, we still offer most people more opportunity for wealth and well-being than at any other time and place in history. We have risen to this position because our nation was founded on the principles laid forth in God's Word. The forces of evil have been held in check by a culture that was based upon the Ten Commandments and a faith in the God of the Bible.

But all of that is rapidly changing, and the civility that once reigned is descending into chaos. At every level of our society we see the same deceptive strategy of the enemy, which is to instill jealousy, envy, and covetousness. Our society is purposefully being fractured by causing people to focus on what someone else has. The American dream of endless opportunity has been replaced by desire to achieve personal gain by depriving someone else. It seems like every aspect of our society has resorted to this deception. Politics has focused on promises of wealth deprived from others. Covetousness has become the tool of business and the economy. An insatiable desire for more and more has consumed the entire society. This insatiable desire for more has undermined even people's ability to think logically. Extreme deficit spending without regard for the consequences has become rampant.

It is the lack of regard for this simple commandment that has for us, in the most privileged generation in history, produced the most spoiled, thankless, irreverent, young people on the planet. Their self-centeredness and self-righteousness have blinded them to the realities of life. The promotion of covetousness is bankrupting this once vibrant country financially, morally, and spiritually. We are beginning to see the debt pile up and the payments of life, liberty, and happiness being extracted from our people.

As with all the commandments we need to hold the high ground to promote its practice. Anything short of "You shall not covet" will fail. Coveting begins in the mind and needs to be restrained at that level. Once it reaches the heart level it begins its destructive work; jealousy, envy, and hatred begin eating away at a person's integrity. From there covetousness begins to exhibit itself in the way we treat other people and then, like a cancer, it affects those around us.

As with all of the commandments, we need to teach it, preach it, and live it. Hold fast to the high ground!

CHAPTER 8

Knowledge, Wisdom, Education

No Compromise

The moral high ground is not something that is obtained by a lifetime of study and work. This high ground is obtained by faith in the Creator of the Universe who has revealed Himself through His Son, Jesus. This is why even a child's understanding can trump the ideals of an old and weathered old man in determining right from wrong. The spiritual laws are as real as the physical laws in God's universe. That is why the Ten Commandments I have just outlined cannot be compromised without a retreat from the high ground. The battle for morality becomes much more difficult once we lose the high ground.

Even more than this, the Ten Commandments form the foundation for our developing understanding of how we are to determine right from wrong. As we face life in this world many times there are situations that arise in which the issue of right and wrong is clouded. It is at these times that it is most important that we do not waver in our confidence of the Word of God. Compromise will leave us on shaky ground and may lead to a slippery slope from which recovery is very difficult.

Knowledge

"The fear of the LORD is the beginning of knowledge; Fools despise wisdom and instruction." (Pr 1:7 NAS95)

"The fear of the LORD is the beginning of wisdom; A good understanding have all those who do [His commandments;] His praise endures forever." (Ps 111:10 NAS95)

Knowledge is an essential element in every aspect of our lives. It has been estimated that until the 19th century knowledge doubled every century. They claim that now human knowledge is doubling every 13 months. They project that human knowledge will soon double every 12 hours. Sounds impressive, doesn't it? Yet with all of that knowledge available, how come so many people do so many stupid things? How did humans survive up until this point in time if they did not have all of our (so-called) knowledge?

Thank God that He programmed into all of his creation some basic knowledge that is necessary for us to even reach the level of where we can begin to learn and accrue knowledge. You know important things like how to breathe and how to suck, things that we recognize as instinct, things we just know. Most of creation, which is usually referred to as "nature", is driven and controlled mostly by the instinct that is programmed into it. The more complex creatures have the ability to learn and adapt to their environment.

But human learning goes to quite another level. We were created for a higher purpose than just to exist. We are never happy simply by existing. We have a desire "to know". One of the problems that arise is that not all knowledge is pleasant, because we live in a fallen world. Knowledge in its purity is truth, and sometimes that is hard to deal with. In our age, knowledge has increased dramatically, but mankind still struggles to find truth. Much of what is presented as knowledge today is merely information, and much of that information is tainted with false ideas and concepts that lead more to confusion than to enlightenment. The questions then remain: What do we know? And how do we know it?

When we accept the Bible as truth we then have a standard by which to judge the tremendous amount of information that we are bombarded with today. No other book can compare to the Bible's history, traditions, and content. But beyond this it has simply proven itself through countless ages to provide the wisdom and answers for life. Many are the honest skeptics who have attempted to disprove the claims of this Book, but ended up proving it to be true and bowing to its wisdom. *"Yet wisdom is vindicated by all her children."* (Lu 7:35 NAS95) We hold the high ground when we determine true knowledge based upon the revelation of Scripture.

Education

There is no doubt that knowledge is liberating. Our founding fathers believed this and attempted to create the most educated society that the world had ever known. Ignorance opens the door to enslavement. Lack of understanding can make you fear that which is beneficial and make you fearless of something that can cause you great harm. Lack of knowledge can make us susceptible to be controlled by evil and evil men. Knowledge is power.

> *"Wisdom [is] the principal thing; [therefore] get wisdom: and with all thy getting get understanding."* (Pr 4:7 AV)

Knowledge can be used for good or for bad. Wisdom insures we handle knowledge properly. Understanding takes us to the next level. God's intent for man was to bring man into the realm of understanding. This is the realm in which purpose, meaning, and beauty fully reveal themselves. We know that in this life we will not fully achieve this because of our physical limitations. But we have glimpses into the mind and heart of God, enough so that we can fully trust His direction and leading.

When our forbears first settled in this country they perceived it as an opportunity to create a society based upon the Word of God. Freed from the close oversight of kings, rulers, and the dictates of man, they chose to follow the commandments from heaven. It was the recognition that the laws of heaven were intended to preserve freedom in a fallen world that inspired the founders to create a society governed by that law. Later the architects of the United States would follow their lead in drawing up our founding documents.

But even in those early settlements they recognized the importance of education if their society, founded on Biblical principles, would be preserved for future generations. All of our early universities were created for this purpose, to train young men in the ways of the Lord. Education was the key to perpetuating a society living freely, protected by God's Law. Even more than this was the hopes that this new society would be an example to the whole world. We were to be as a city on a hill, a light to the world, promoting the Gospel of Jesus Christ, the gospel of peace.

Inasmuch as that vision was followed, this society flourished. The foundation that was laid in many of those early colonies set the tone for the emerging republic that followed. All of our founding documents reflect the acknowledgment and reliance on God and His Law. Early in the development of our government the importance of education again rose to the forefront. The Bible was approved as a textbook, for all our early leaders recognized its importance in maintaining the foundational basis of our society and government.

How times have changed! How could anyone have imagined that the very laws that were created to protect and defend our foundation would be twisted to remove that foundation from the educational system created to perpetuate and protect it for future generations? How could this happen? Subtly the focus was redirected away from that which was most important, the foundation.

Remember: ***"The fear of the LORD is the beginning of knowledge;*** … (Pr 1:7 NAS95) When a people lose their fear of God, then gratitude and thanksgiving are replaced with pride and arrogance. Such was the case as the intellectual world attempted to rationalize God out of existence. We all know where this led, but most people are unwilling to acknowledge why it happened. The 20th century was the bloodiest in all of human history. Countless millions of people were slaughtered and tortured. What happened to the city on a hill, the light to the world? That city was besieged, attacked from every side. The educational system was hit hardest. Many are the brave soldiers that stood their ground, but eventually the educational system was infiltrated by those who sought to destroy its foundation.

Most of the benefits of education are revealed in the future. Our founding fathers knew this. Evil men understand this. An entire culture can change direction in one generation through the education of its youth. What you teach your youth is crucial for the future of that society. But you simply cannot hold the high ground in any discussion about education if you exclude God and the Law of God. The fear of God is the beginning of knowledge, wisdom, and understanding. Anything less is a perversion of truth and always leads to destruction.

Several years ago I stood before the school board in our small town. A biology teacher was removed from his job because every year he deviated from the evolutionary textbook for two days of the year to present the concept of intelligent design. He had been doing this for ten years, but now one student and the ACLU had threatened the school district with a lawsuit if this process was not stopped.

I knew that at that time almost every board member and the superintendent were members in Christian Churches. I challenged them, asking them how they could believe in God and yet insist that their children be taught that they are just a product of time and a series of accidents. I stood and spoke to them, wrote letters to them, and a huge community meeting was organized, all to no avail.

The answer I received was that it was imperative for them to avoid a lawsuit, and most important was that the educational process not be interrupted. One bold member, who was a dairy farmer, likened the situation to his business. He said, "The most important thing I do is milk my cows. In the same way it is most important that we make sure the education of our children goes on uninterrupted."

I countered his comment by saying, "You are wrong; the most important thing is what you feed your cows, because if they do not get the proper food there will not be any milk. You have all focused on education and education is important, but the most important thing is what we teach our children, not simply that we teach them. Education will be counterproductive if what we teach our children is not true."

Fear won out and the high ground of truth and integrity in education was lost in my small home town and everywhere else in America. Today a large portion of the students in our town end up in an alternative school so that we can pretend that they have received an education. The very foundation of our society, and knowledge of it, has been outlawed from our educational system. It is no wonder that our society is imploding since we removed its foundation from our public school system, distorting our principles, laws, and causing even a rewrite of our history.

The battle for what our children are taught continues to be fought with high sounding phrases like: "No child left behind", or "Common Core". Discussions on every level argue what children really need to know to flourish in our society. Some argue for knowledge without morality. Some argue for morality without authority. But if we are to preserve this nation and its government that have proven to be the most successful in history, then we cannot lose the high ground concerning education.

> **"Our Constitution was made only for a moral and religious people". It is wholly inadequate to the government of any other."** *John Adams*

If we do not teach our children, first and foremost, a reverence for God and His Commandments, then our Constitution will not be adequate to govern their affairs. If we do not use God's Word as blueprint for their education, then we will not preserve a society that upholds the sanctity of the life of each individual citizen and their God-given rights.

CHAPTER 9
The Distinctions of God

The Boundaries He Has Established

"Then God said, "Let there be light"; and there was light. And God saw that the light was good; and God separated the light from the darkness. And God called the light day, and the darkness He called night. And there was evening and there was morning, one day." (Ge 1:3-5 NAS)

Genesis reveals to us the intentional order and design of our Creator. In every phase of creation week God sets boundaries and distinctions that maintain His order and beauty. Separations of; light and darkness, day and night, the waters above and waters below, plants and their distinct kinds, plants and animals, animals and their distinct kinds, man and animals, male and female, and God and man, all created in symbiotic relationship to maintain and perpetuate a perfect creation.

God and Man

"And the serpent said to the woman, "You surely shall not die! "For God knows that in the day you eat from it your eyes will be opened, and

you will be like God, knowing good and evil.""
(Ge 3:4-5 NAS)

Satan lied to Eve in an attempt to convince her that they could be as God Himself. That lie resulted in man's deception and fall. Not only did he fail to ascend to God's level, but he descended to a lower level bringing corruption upon all of creation.

One of Satan's strategies to pervert and destroy God's creation and disrupt His plan is to blur the distinctions and boundaries in God's creation that provide security and order. In the first attack in the Garden of Eden, Satan proposed that created man could be equal with God. Although man had been created in the image and likeness of God, there will always be a vast distinction between the Creator and His creation. This is a boundary that cannot be breached even though Satan desires it to be so. Satan desires to be like the most high and has planted that seed of rebellion and desire in the imagination of man. Satan will never cross that boundary and neither will man.

Reality set in swiftly as Adam and Eve partook of the forbidden fruit. They had not become as God, but they had acquired knowledge of good and evil. It merely took the presence of God to clarify the distinction between the creator and the created. The voice of the deceiver was silent and Adam and Eve stood before God naked and ashamed. They had attempted the impossible, but man cannot become like God. Man had violated his boundary bringing death and destruction on himself and the earth with which he had been entrusted.

Man's sin did not alter God or the Laws that govern God's creation. Man's sin altered his relationship with God. But God in his mercy has a plan of redemption for those who are willing to put their trust in Him. Reconciling man back to the intended fellowship arrangement is God's intent. God has provided everything necessary to restore the perfect relationship between God and man. The only thing that remains for reconciliation to be complete is man's submission to the Law of God.

But through deception and pride man continues to try to breach that divide between man and God by attempting to ascend to that throne himself. The lie that was planted in the Garden continues to deceive. The revelation of God is clear, but through foolish speculation man's heart is darkened.

> *"because that which is known about God is evident within them; for God made it evident to them. For since the creation of the world His invisible attributes, His eternal power and divine nature, have been clearly seen, being understood through what has been made, so that they are without excuse. For even though they knew God, they did not honor Him as God, or give thanks; but they became futile in their speculations, and their foolish heart was darkened. Professing to be wise, they became fools, and exchanged the glory of the incorruptible God for an image in the form of corruptible man and of birds and four-footed animals and crawling creatures."*
> (Ro 1:19-23 NAS)

Sin separated man from fellowship with God. But the revelation of God and His eternal power and divine nature are revealed in His creation for all to see. Rather than trusting God's promise and plan of reconciliation, mankind rebels. Rebellion spawns the need for self-deception promoted through imagination and conjecture. In man's attempt to reconcile man to god he tries to bring god down to our level. Man creates god in his own image, that of sinful man. From there god is depicted as birds and four footed creatures, and then as crawling creepy creatures. There has been no end to what man has in times and places chosen to worship as god, even plants, trees, mountains, the sun, moon, and stars. Man has not only chosen to worship the creation instead of the creator, but has created images of these things and worshiped those images.

> **"Remember the former things long past, For I am God, and there is no other; I am God, and there is no one like Me,"...** (Isa 46:9 NAS)

Why am I spending so much time on this point? Because recognizing God in His distinctive role as creator of all things is the most important point of all. Blurring that distinction or the ramifications of His position in the slightest opens our imaginations to perverted images of God. If we continue to read Romans, Paul expounds upon the extent of the perversion of all that was created holy. Once man blurs or disregards the revelation of God, he opens the door for corruption to invade.

The distinction of God from all of creation, including mankind and angelic beings, needs to be foremost in our minds when seeking truth and understanding. The high moral ground is established by God alone. That is why any discussion concerning morality we must argue foremost from that perspective. Recognizing the vast difference between man and God is just the first of many distinctions and boundaries that are essential.

Angels and Devils

Anchoring our understanding of God as revealed to us through Christ Jesus, we can separate truth from myth and imagination. Because sin separated man from God, the spiritual realm became fertile ground for man's imagination. Man's spirit is bound to his mortal body unlike the spirits of angels and demons. God is also a spirit, but unlike any other spirit, He alone is immortal, having neither beginning nor end.

> *"who alone possesses immortality and dwells in unapproachable light; whom no man has seen or can see. To Him be honor and eternal dominion! Amen."* (1Ti 6:16 NAS)

Man's sin created a spiritual divide between man and God. Nevertheless a spiritual connection was maintained through sacrificial offerings of animals until in the fullness of time Christ Jesus became the Lamb that would take away the sins of the world. In spite of God's provision the spirit of rebellion still lies within man. At the heart of that rebellion is the pride and jealousy provoked by the lie of Satan. Just as Eve was deceived into believing that the Law of God was intended to withhold something good from her, so people are convinced of this lie today. But even in this state of rebellion man's spirit still longs for a spiritual connection. Satan and those spirits that are in rebellion seek to take advantage of this vulnerability in man and suggest an alternative connection.

God is in a class by Himself. Neither angels or devils or Satan is like God. Every spirit except God has had a beginning and will ultimately have to give answer to Him and be judged by Him. That is why the separations and distinctions that God has established are so important and to be honored by those of us who are His creation. But when people distance themselves from the Word of God their concept of the spiritual world becomes distorted. The pronounced difference between God and the other spiritual beings gets blurred. In their ignorance they open themselves up to spiritual connections with those spirits that are in rebellion to God.

Satan's attack on God's creation has often been to blur the distinction and separations that God has established, knowing that when we cross these lines it will bring about destruction. The deceptive notion that Satan is like God opens the door for all the other perversions. Those who follow Satan's spiritual leading become the tools he uses to spread his lies and destructive heresies.

Good and Evil

I realize that there is a fair amount of repetition in this section from what I have already written. But I think it necessary to look at these issues from the perspective of the perversion of the boundaries that God had put in place. It is in the blurring of the distinction between God and His creation that opens the door for the blurring of what is good and what is evil. In our world good and evil live alongside of each other. Humans were created in the image and likeness of God, but since Adam's sin we are also born in sin and often violate God's Law. We cannot say that people are good, because often they are not good. Neither can I agree that people are totally depraved, because often they do good things, and most people want to be good.

> *"And a certain ruler questioned Him, saying, "Good Teacher, what shall I do to inherit eternal life?" And Jesus said to him, "Why do you call Me good? No one is good except God alone. "You know the commandments, 'DO NOT COMMIT ADULTERY, DO NOT MURDER, DO NOT STEAL, DO NOT BEAR FALSE WITNESS, HONOR YOUR FATHER AND MOTHER.'"'* (Lu 18:18-20 NAS)

God alone is good. His unique position as creator of all things gives Him alone the authority to determine what is good. This is where the Law of God comes in, it defines "good" for us. If sin had not entered this world we would be good and know only good. But evil desire has been planted in us and this is why we needed a Savior, to deliver us from evil. It is the blurring of the distinction between good and evil that is instrumental in enticing us to sin. We often do things that we think will be good for us, ignoring or rationalizing how our actions will affect others.

What I am trying to tell you is that it is only in adhering to the Law of God that we can claim the high moral ground on any subject dealing with our character or behavior. The reason you will be lured to argue your stance from a lower level is because at those lower levels it is easier to blur that pronounced distinction between good and evil. Behavior can seem good on an individual level, but from God's perspective the ramification for the effect on others render that behavior evil.

The worldly doctrine that truth is relative has also blurred the concepts of good and evil. Satan is having a heyday with this by inspiring young people to rise up and promote destructive behaviors. When the line between good and evil becomes blurred, then anything and everything can be in some measure considered good. For those on this road to self-destruction, the only thing that is truly evil in their mind is for someone to give knowledge of the Creator's line of division between good and evil.

Male and Female

> *"And He answered and said, "Have you not read, that He who created them from the beginning MADE THEM MALE AND FEMALE,"* (Mt 19:4 NAS)

I do not think that there has ever been a time in history when Satan's influence has progressed as fast or as far in blurring the clear distinctions that God has established. A few years ago no one could have imagined the distinction between male and female being blurred. As with all the distinctions that God has established, you have to ignore what is clearly revealed to not see the defining attributes that define male and female.

To the untrained eye, among baby chicks it is hard to tell the roosters from the hens. But by the time they mature it is usually hard to ignore the distinct differences. The roosters crow and the hens lay eggs, among other differences. Even these bird brains seem to get this figured out. The fact that there is a strong drive in our society to blur the distinction of male and female is mind boggling. The fact that the concept of a sexless society has progressed this far in my lifetime is mind boggling, not just because it is my lifetime, but because we live in an age of advanced scientific knowledge.

It is true that there is more to us as humans than our biology. But our biology is probably the clearest indication that a man is not a woman and a woman is not a man. We have even come to learn that that distinction is clear even in the makeup of each of our trillions of cells. We know that women think differently than men. The two different sexes are wired differently and are regulated differently by different chemicals within the body. So why is our society trying to erase their natural distinctions?

Again, we are confronted with the lies and distortions intended to fuel pride, envy, and greed. Just as Satan tempted Eve in the Garden of Eden that she could find fulfillment in being as God, so the temptation follows in this venue. The lie of Satan is that happiness and fulfillment can come through equality. Satan desired to be equal with God or the same as God. To some degree he has achieved that role amongst those spirits and humans who honor him. But what is the result of his exultation to that role? God in that role is a creator, life giver, and bene-factor. Satan in that role brings death and destruction seeking to devour that which God has created. Having had an honored position Satan was not content, but through envy and pride he sought to be equal with God. In an attempt to cross the boundary of creator and creation Satan compromised all that was created in him as good and became evil, and an influence for evil, in all who follow him.

God created men and women to be distinctly different. Those differences were not intended to create rivalry but were designed to be complimentary. God's intent was that the two would be united and become as one. Their oneness then becomes the foundation for family, community, and country. But when individuals violate God's Law, the Law of Love, then problems arise and conflict comes within this sacred union. If the rift that results is not mended, that which was joined as one becomes broken.

Logically, if we have something that is broken that needs to be mended, we would do best to consult the plans of the designer to clarify how it was originally put together. But we now live in a society that has distanced themselves from their Creator. When we ignore the instruction manual, it opens the door for other suggestions. The first suggestion is that there was a design problem. That opens the door for a variety of solutions that have wreaked havoc on the sacred union of man and woman.

One of the tools the enemy has used to destroy this aspect of God's creation is the use of the concept of equality. The concept of equality sounds so good, and it is if applied correctly. The Scripture teaches us that we are all created in the image of God and that God is not a respecter of persons. God's love and justice are distributed equally for every person. In other words, we are all of equal value in God's eyes. But the way that God does that is not the same for each of us, because God had created us with differences. Obviously, God likes variety, because we come in different colors, sizes, and abilities. But the distinctions of the different sexes define the definite roles intended for us to fulfill His purpose. Male and female are of equal value, but they are not the same.

The rejection of God's instruction for fair treatment of males and females has resulted in a quest to make the sexes equal. The fact is that equal respect for each other requires respect and appreciation for the distinct differences between male and female. With the breakdown of the complimentary relationship of male and female in marriage, the door swung wide open for adversarial roles. In some cases people tried to look and act like the other sex. In other cases people used their differences to take advantage of the other sex. Not only do these approaches fail to bring fair treatment, they end up making the problem worse and create a multitude of problems in their wake.

Consider this simple illustration: we have two arms and two hands that are complimentary to each other. Each side is just as valuable and important as the other side, but they are not equal. Both arms are facing opposite directions. For most people one arm is dominate; you are right handed or left handed. If you still think that they are equal, then try to imagine the difficulties that would arise if you had two left arms instead of a right and a left.

Man's attempt to dissolve God's distinct created differences between male and female has had disastrous consequences. Both sexes have suffered devaluation. In a sense, it is like trying to hang a left arm on the right side of the body and the right arm on the left. Either one or both will have to adapt to create the illusion of equality. In the process you will mask the differences that make the sexes complimentary. Marriage becomes unbalanced and awkward.

When the sexes are considered to be equivalent, then your sexuality does not really matter that much. This opens the door for the acceptance of same sex-marriage and all the transgender experimentation that people can generate. This experimentation has resulted in several classes of people trying to live illogical lifestyles.

I could argue the logic of God's creative genius all day concerning the complementary nature of male and female. From our aesthetics to science the awesomeness of our human design is undisputable. Why would anyone want to mess with the complementary design of the sexes? Why would you even want to make male and female interchangeable? You can never make a male as female as a female and vice versa, so why would you try?

Some have been convinced that there will be some benefit in making male and female interchangeable. By getting people to focus on what they do not have often makes it possible to exchange the truth for a lie. The distinction between male and female is essential for God's creation to operate correctly. All of God's creation was made to be logical and orderly. The distinction between male and female, because it is high on God's created order, is of great importance. Obviously, the higher on the created order something is, the greater affect on the whole when that orderliness is compromised. Therefore convincing people to compromise the male/female distinction is a devastating blow to God's created order. Satan's tactics seem to be to distract people from the love and goodness that flow from created order and design, and to imagine a benefit that can come by destroying that order.

But what about those who have violated this taboo and claim it to be beneficial for them? Certainly it would be foolish to argue our point from their narrow perspective. Rather, we need to back up to get a broader view and consider the cost of their supposed benefit. To start with, if we use a substitute for that which was originally designed, we are deprived of the real thing. Secondly, you risk damaging that which is abused. The costs in this case are both personal and societal and are robbing society of that which is good and beneficial. Likewise, there is medical, psychological, and social damage that affects on a personal and societal level.

This is not one of those subjects that I want to go into with explicit details, for several reasons. So, to explain the imbalance of benefit to cost, I will use this simple illustration. My job required that I be trained in fighting fires. Every year we would receive refresher training, suiting up and fighting actual fires on a fire training ground. Often our gloves ended up in a big mixed-up pile and we would have to make sure we got gloves that fit, and that we had a right and left glove. The easy way would have been just to grab a couple of gloves and go; the benefit was we would get a good seat on the bus. But if we ended up with two left-handed gloves, then handling the fire hoses for the next couple of hours was a big pain. I always searched until I found a glove that fit well for each of my hands. Rushing to try to get a good seat on the bus for a ride that lasted 5 minutes just was not worth the benefits of good fitting gloves for the next couple of hours fighting fire.

I know this is just a simple illustration, but if this logic makes sense for my fire fighting training, then imagine how much sense it would make if I was fighting an actual out of control fire. Failure to use the proper equipment could result in me being injured. Worse yet, it could affect the ability of the entire fire fighting crew and anyone else effected by the fire.

When we are talking about sexuality, the roles of male and female, we are talking about something that is sacred. The proper union of male and female is foundational to the purpose and function of mankind. This union was intended to also provide joy, comfort, and a multitude of blessings. Even beyond all of this it provides us with understanding of the depth of the fellowship that God intends to have with us. This relationship is intended to teach us the root of the character of God, which is love.

The costs of violating the division of male and female are tremendous and the benefits are few and fleeting.

Man and Animal

"All flesh is not the same flesh, but there is one flesh of men, and another flesh of beasts, and another flesh of birds, and another of fish."
(1Co 15:39 NAS)

"Then God said, "Let Us make man in Our image, according to Our likeness; and let them rule over the fish of the sea and over the birds of the sky and over the cattle and over all the earth, and over every creeping thing that creeps on the earth." And God created man in His own image, in the image of God He created him; male and female He created them." (Ge 1:26-27 NAS)

The division between man and woman is a division between two sexes of equal value. Men and women were intended to be unified in an equal bond. Together they were created in the image and likeness of God. But the distinction between Man and animal is entirely a different thing. People in their created order were to have dominion over all the other created creatures. The very nature of all these things attests to the revelation God has given in the Scriptures concerning the relationship of man to beast.

As people drift from the testimony of Scripture and science, they are drawn into the elusions of the imagination through the influence of Satan. History is full of examples of how people have come to worship beasts and images of beasts. Man's descent into his evil imagination results in a deep and dark bondage. Under this bondage of darkness inspired by that creature that was revealed in the Garden of Eden, Man's actions often reflected those of ignorant and wild beasts. Man's creative abilities and intelligence were suppressed by the destructive nature of this dark bondage. People warred against people seeking to rise above their fellow man, providing a history of the rise and fall of nations.

The relatively recent advent of the enlightenment seemed to for a while lift people through the intellect to recognize the superiority of Mankind over the animals. This period of enlightenment produced an explosion of knowledge, science, and an industrial revolution. Today the root cause of the enlightenment is often overlooked. It was the spread of Christianity that really was at the heart of this revolution. It was Christianity that again brought a level of clarity and understanding of the world around us. It was Christianity that clarified those divisions in God's creation that are necessary for order. A world drifting away from God was blurring the distinctions between God, men, animals, and nature. Recognizing the God-given order allowed men to again take dominion of those earthly things with which he was originally entrusted with. Myths, religions, and spiritual influences had suppressed man's ability to see clearly and distinguish between the truth and a lie.

The enlightenment had a two prong effect. There was an explosion of knowledge that is continuing even now. But as with every good that comes from above, if it is used within the bounds of the Law of God it brings great blessing, but if those laws are ignored it brings a curse. The access to this new knowledge fed the sinful pride that lies within mankind, and in greed and arrogance people rose up denying the source of knowledge and truth.

The result is that we have two camps. One group of people becomes increasingly aware of the marvelous beauty and design that speaks of a loving Creator. The other group blinds themselves by their denial of a creator. Denying the wisdom revealed in all of creation, they seek to rule the world inspired by their own evil imaginations and the lies of the god of this world. The enlightenment brought peace and war, prosperity and poverty, knowledge and ignorance, and wisdom and foolishness.

In spite of our high tech age we are witnessing a descent of mankind from the dignified position to which God intended to elevate us. There are now those who, as in times past, place mankind with or below the level of unintelligent beasts and creeping creatures. In spite of God's revelations they choose to worship the creation rather than the Creator. They stoop to the lowest of the low, the earth itself, and worship the rocks and gas as their mother and giver of life.

It is in this cultural environment that the line between people and animals is being blurred to the point their lives and existence has become equal in value. Let me again remind you that this is another one of God's distinct boundaries that are intended to keep his creative order and bless mankind. Even the seemingly innocent personification of animals in stories and film are playing into this deception. As cities and technology have isolated people from the realities of the real world, their precepts of reality and imagination are blurred in this area too.

Dennis Prager has for years asked young people this question: If your dog and a stranger were both drowning and you could only save one which one, would you choose? Increasingly more people would choose the dog or are undecided. Today the news of the death and mutilation of seven cats has trumped the murder of people in our streets. Thirty thousand dollars has been offered for a reward for the capture of the cat killer, and a special task force has been assigned to find the killer.

Meanwhile, the abortion of innocent humans is presented as health care and a right that every woman should have.

The high moral ground is that God created man in His image and likeness. God breathed His breath into man and man became a living soul. Man sinned and brought a curse on all of creation, but God through Christ Jesus provided a means of redemption. Animals were created as an element of our environment that was prepared for mankind, a wonderful and precious blessing, but not an equal to humans. God seeks to elevate, but man chooses to descend.

Blurring the Lines

I have touched on some of the major divisions of God's creation. When there is an attempt to dissolve the lines of distinction that God intended, the misuse always creates problems. There are many other categories and sub-categories that I have not mentioned that are often abused and misused that result in a disruption in God's created order. The created division of God's order cannot be changed, but through abuse and misuse people can blur the lines. This disruption of the harmony of God's creation always has dire consequences. Today we are witnessing these abuses at an unprecedented level. Modern science and technology have allowed us to create incredible illusions that appear to be real and functional on their face. Man has blurred the lines but reality remains unchanged. Eventually every man will come face to face with reality as we face the Creator and are required to give answers for our rebellion and disregard for the order of God and His creation.

CHAPTER 10

The Sanctity of Life

Life

Life still remains a mystery. We can analyze life; determine what it is made out of, and even get down to its atomic structure. But we still do not know why or how it becomes alive. The mystery deepens when we study ourselves, the pinnacle of God's creation, made in His image and likeness. The human spirit, our souls, our emotions, imaginations, and desires, enhance our physical bodies in ways that seem to defy our understanding. Instinctively we protect our physical life, but our soul and spirit elevate the joy of living far beyond simply the physical. The sanctity of human life then has become basic in what we have come to call a civilized society.

Whether we are considering human behavior or simply life itself the Bible is the only source that can give us a coherent understanding and a guideline for determining right from wrong. There has never been a time in history when mankind has had our knowledge of the intricacies involved in a person's life. Never has there been a time in history when the verification of the wisdom of the Scripture has been as obvious as it is today with our abilities to search it out. Here in America we live in a society that was founded on the principles of life and liberty drawn from the Holy Scripture. Now, at a time of great enlightenment, people are abandoning those principles that had opened the doors of opportunities for all people. Choosing to hide among the contradicting philosophies, Americans are forsaking the clear vision that brought us together. The subject of life itself reveals their willful ignorance and abandoning of reason to fulfill their petty, self-centered desires.

Abortion

We now know from scientific discovery that all of mankind is from a single family. We now know that there is only one race of humans. We all know that we are more than just a physical body and have a soul and spirit. We know exactly when life begins in a woman's womb. We know how and why life begins in a woman's womb. All these things were revealed to us in the Scripture long before we scientifically were able to prove them to be true.

> *"I will give thanks to You, for I am fearfully and wonderfully made; Wonderful are Your works, And my soul knows it very well. My frame was not hidden from You, When I was made in secret, [And] skillfully wrought in the depths of the earth; Your eyes have seen my unformed substance; And in Your book were all written The days that were ordained [for me,] When as yet there was not one of them."*
> (Ps 139:14-16 NAS95)

We now know scientifically that from the time of conception the information about every detail of our physical bodies was determined and designed to develop to maturity. As of yet, man is not able to measure the soul or fully understand the spirit of man. But we know from the Scripture that God looks on and acknowledges our individuality before our substance took form.

Justification for abortion has been argued in spite of increased knowledge, not because of it. The reality that abortion is legal upon demand in America reveals the power of sin in people's hearts over the power of reason. A woman's rights or a woman's health are reasons against abortion, not for it. The high moral ground in this issue is found in truth and righteousness. It is found in the sanctity of human life and the command from heaven that you shall not murder.

The Birds and the Bees

Why would a mother want to kill her baby? Why would she choose to end the life of her baby? Should she have the right to make the choice to terminate the life of her unborn child? If we sink to the level of a mother's rights and choice, then our arguments do not adequately address their demands. But if we defend a pro-life position from the high ground using God's Word and the revelations of science, then rights and choice come into perspective. After all, what about the health of the babies and their rights and choices?

Every conception is a result of choice. It is difficult to imagine in an educated society such as ours that a person would come to maturity without acquiring the knowledge of how babies are conceived. Ignorance would not be a reason to justify murder anyway. Babies do not just happen, but are the result of people's choices. It is at this juncture that the rights of the woman are to be honored. The union of a man and a woman is to be a result of both of their consents. If their choice results in the conception of a new soul, then it is also both of their responsibilities to take care of that baby. The arguments of rights and choice become mute at this point recognizing that they have exercised their right and made a choice. If the result of their choice has produced a human life, why does the mother have the right to take this person's life? Why does she alone have the choice of life or death in regards to their baby? Why does her choice trump the laws of God and of the United States?

Of course, the issue of rape will arise, for there are cases where a rape results in a pregnancy. But we have already established that the baby that is forming is a human being recognized by God. Would we be justified to kill this baby because of the sins of the father? Of course, the sins of the father do not justify the killing of an innocent life. Rather, it should compel us to extend help and comfort to this mother and her baby.

Deception

Those who argue for abortion try to do so claiming the high moral ground. That is why they form their arguments around concern for the mother, totally ignoring concern or even acknowledgement of the baby being killed. The fact of the matter is that abortion is not good for the mother either. Even if a woman allows herself to be convinced that what is being aborted is not really a person, she will suffer emotionally and physically because the process of life was disrupted within her. My dad once told me that when a baby is born a mother is born.

I witnessed the truth of this statement when my son was born and my wife became a mother. When a baby is aborted the process of becoming a mother is also disrupted causing pain and suffering even beyond the physical. Emotional scars are harder to heal than physical ones.

The categorization of abortion as an element of women's health is totally irrational. Pregnancy is not a disease. A developing baby is not an appendage of the mother, but is a separate individual. Being pregnant is not unhealthy. Pregnancy is a drain on a woman's system, but then so is exercise or work or taking care of children after they are born. The fact is; abortion is detrimental to women's health, physically, mentally, and emotionally.

Roots

Abortion is the killing of an unborn child. The brutality of this practice is even accented when it is visualized while being performed in the latter stages of the child's development. The fact that many view this horrible procedure as a solution points to the fact that there is an earlier problem, the problem of an unwanted pregnancy. That problem is usually the product of unwise choices. Unwise choices are usually the results of ignorance or simply ignoring knowledge and wisdom. The underlying problem can be lack of education or willful ignorance. Sometimes you simply have to go back to the beginning to understand the real root of the problem. We will never stop abortions without addressing the issues that lead up to people's decisions to abort their babies.

As already stated, the fear of God is the beginning of knowledge, wisdom, and understanding. The laws of the universe reveal the character and nature of God Himself. When we ignore these laws there are consequences.

In the Beginning

> *"But from the beginning of creation, [God] MADE THEM MALE AND FEMALE. "FOR THIS REASON A MAN SHALL LEAVE HIS FATHER AND MOTHER, AND THE TWO SHALL BECOME ONE FLESH; so they are no longer two, but one flesh. "What therefore God has joined together, let no man separate."* (Mr 10:6-9 NAS95)

God created an ordered universe in which all things functioned harmoniously. It is Man's choices that disrupt that harmony and create problems. It only makes things worse when people promote solutions that are intended to justify their bad choices. These bad choices and even worse solutions multiply suffering rather than relieving it. Abortion is presented as a solution. If we eliminate the problem, then the evil solution disappears by itself. But to do this we have to go back to the beginning.

The creation account does not reveal all the detailed intricacies of life, but we are given the important information necessary for our understanding of our role in this plan of God. God made one man and one woman, separate individuals, intended to be joined together as one unit. The ramification of this fundamental unit extends throughout all of creation from its perfect beginning, to the fall, and through to its redemption. The health of the family unit is necessary for the health of a society, a country, and the world we live in. If we are talking women's health, then this is where we need to start.

Love Makes the World Go Around

God chose to make just one man and one woman. In so doing He preserved His purpose and intent with clarity, one man, one woman, for life. Man has tried other options with disastrous results. Sin, the violation of God's Law, resulted in God having to spell His Law out for us, and He has through his Holy Scripture. When man has followed the wisdom of God's Word, then God has blessed. Natural attractions lead us in the right direction, obedience to God's Word keeps us on the correct path. Because our culture was based upon the fear of God and reverence to His Word, fundamental truth was even reflected in children's playground taunts.

> *"First comes love, then comes marriage, then comes Bobby with a baby carriage."*

Love is the main ingredient in that healthy relationship between a man and a woman that results in a healthy marriage. But if we are to hold to the high moral ground in this discussion we have to view it from a Biblical perspective. If we chose to let Hollywood and the media define love for us we won't have the substance to create a good marriage relationship, or any other good loving relationship. In this self-centered, sinful world many of the important aspects of love need to be learned, not everything comes naturally.

C. S. Lewis, in his book, "The Four Loves", points out that there are actually four Greek words in the New Testament that we translated into English as "love". Besides helping us understand Scripture better we can also see how easily the concepts of love can be confusing in our culture. To add to the confusion in our language, having sex has been equated with making love.

Briefly described, the four loves are:

Storge: Affection Love – enjoying something or someone

Phileo: Friendship Love – Friendship love, arising out of companionship, common interest

Eros: Romantic Love – emotional, most felt, being in love

Agape: Divine Love – It gives and asks nothing in return – unselfish love

In the ideal marriage all of these loves come together. When we are looking for solutions to the problems that arise because of the relationships between men and women the answer lies in the agape form of love. This is a love that is not contingent upon emotional feelings, changing interests, or preferences. It is under the control of a person's choice, commitment, and resolve. It is the love that is necessary to honestly exchange the wedding vows.

"First comes love". For the Christian, love is to be present in all of our relationships, loving God and loving our neighbor. Charity begins at home. This is where we first experience it and this is where we learn to practice it. Charity is, of course, that Agape Love that stems from the divine, reminding us where we came from.

Marriage

"But from the beginning of creation, [God] MADE THEM MALE AND FEMALE. "FOR THIS REASON A MAN SHALL LEAVE HIS FATHER AND MOTHER, AND THE TWO SHALL BECOME ONE FLESH; so they are no longer two, but one flesh."
(Mr 10:6-8 NAS95)

"Then comes marriage". Love is a requirement for marriage, but marriage is not a requirement for love. The love that is required for marriage is agape love. The love that usually inspires marriage is eros. A perfect marriage has all four types of love. Situations and events may cause the first three loves to fluctuate, but agape love must remain steady, and can if we will.

The reason for marriage is because God made us male and female. From the beginning, and until very recent history, everyone knew this simple fact. The definition of the word "marriage" in the English dictionary is: The union of a man and a woman. But through a barrage of information the highest court in our land ignored the facts and redefined the word marriage to be able to include unions between two people of the same sex. This issue was debated on every level, from the perspectives of love, to feelings, to possessions. This is a sad reflection on our judicial system and especially the high court. To accommodate the emotional appeal and social pressure the court ignored the logical and legal aspects of the case. The high ground perspective is simply that the reason for marriage is because God made us male and female.

The battle for marriage was first lost in the classroom, in the movies, and in the media. These are areas in which the issue could be presented from an emotional perspective without rebuttal. These are areas that do not allow for honest debate and can press their dogmas through the high cards of power and money. It was because of their confidence in the emotional manipulation of the public that judges have become bold in issuing tyrannical rulings. By leaving the high ground of logic and law, the focus became centered on the feelings of a minority group. This distraction allowed them to overturn every one of the thousands of laws dealing with marriage. If you think it through, the implications are staggering. Their rulings to include same sex couples under the marriage laws rendered God's Law and the Constitution of the United States as mute points.

Even worse than what has been done in the courts is how this issue has infiltrated the churches of America. When "Christians" allow themselves to be drawn down to the world's level to discuss or debate truth, they lose the high ground that they are responsible for holding. Marriage is not about who you love. That argument falls flat before it leaves a person's mouth. You can and should love you mother, father, brother, sister, neighbor, and maybe even your dog or horse. No matter what degree of love you have for any of these, you should not become one flesh with any of them.

If we want to hold the high moral ground we have to stick with Scripture. If there are those who indeed care about truth we need to have honest discussions. Same-sex marriage is not about love as I have pointed out. It is not about sex, although this is how they define their relationship. For some of them it is about finding acceptance for their life style. Certainly most of them do not feel the need for marriage before they have sex. And marriage is not necessary for inheritance or property issues. Legal contracts and wills can cover all these issues.

The reason for marriage is because God made us male and female. It was God's judgment that it was not good for man to be alone. Woman was created for this purpose, that man would not be alone and would have someone to walk alongside of him. She was created complementary to man so that in coming together with him they would have offspring. The two are to leave father and mother and become one flesh, one unit, the foundation for family. Children are the tangible results of their oneness.

But what is the reason for same sex- marriage? Is it so that same sex-couples can have the same benefits as married couples, and then with everything being equal, they can be just as happy and fulfilled? But could they be fulfilled, or would they be fulfilled, seeing that some relationships lack the feminine and others the masculine? Or is it to show that man does not need woman and woman does not need man? Saying it, does not make it so. Legal and or social affirmation does not make it so.

The reasons for same sex-couples relationships to be categorized as marriage are not the same as reasons for opposite-sex marriage. If we hold to the high moral ground and follow this discussion to where it leads, we will end up contrasting the good and holy with the perverted and profane. The simple answer that the reason for marriage is because God made us male and female has tremendous ramifications. It would take a large volume to fully reveal the marvelous complimentary nature of the proper union of male and female. But even a superficial glance can detect the physical, mental, and spiritual differences from the male and female intended to be complimentary. On the other hand, fantastic imagination and innovation are required to consummate same sex-couples.

The end of a matter reveals much of the purpose of its functions. Marriage resulted in the creation of the families of earth. Marriage produces a balanced family structure that becomes the building block of moral societies. On the other hand, same-sex relationships do not produce children. Through the perversion of the natural functions they have created their own unique physical problems, mental issues, and diseases.

The Fruit of Marriage

"And then comes Bobby with a baby carriage".

"Did not the Lord God make you one? Your life and breath belong to him. And why did he make you one? because he wants godly offspring." ... (Mal 2:15 KJV_2011)

There are numerous benefits of a good marriage (one that honors God and His Law) for a man and a woman. But the fruit of a godly marriage is godly children. Likewise, the fruit of a godless marriage is godless children. There is no greater advantage to children than the environment of a godly home and a loving father and mother. It was the recognition of this fact that inspired most of our early laws pertaining to marriage. Laws were created to encourage and provide advantages for families raising children. Those laws were turned on their ear with the redefining of marriage.

Children are the most vulnerable in society. They are reliant upon the adult world to provide for them. Because we as humans are more than just physical beings, children need more than just food, clothing, and shelter. Children need love, instruction, and discipline, for they are not born with knowledge, wisdom, and understanding. Children's innocent enquiring nature makes them highly susceptible to be influenced by adult behavior, education, media, and the arts. Because we live in a world affected by sin, this includes the good, the bad, and the ugly. The union of a man and a woman in marriage was intended to not only produce fruit, but to be the avenue of provision to bring that fruit to maturity.

Children represent the future. God's intention was that they would be the fruit of marriage. Many children today are the fruit of people's self-centered desires. These children that are deprived of family are at the mercy of a morally declining society and its influences. The result is an increasingly large population of young people who are mentally and morally retarded, people who never seem to fully mature mentally and spiritually. This population is easily manipulated by unscrupulous tyrants who lure them with promises of unrealistic expectations. If this is not soon arrested the hopes for the future of our nation are dismal as we descend into the abyss of self-destruction.

> *"For I have chosen him, in order that he may command his children and his household after him to keep the way of the LORD by doing righteousness and justice; in order that the LORD may bring upon Abraham what He has spoken about him."* (Ge 18:19 NAS)

"Children are our future", has been the beginning statement of many discussions which seek to convince people of a specific plan or action. People's love and concern for children is admirable. But there are a lot of different ideas about what would be best for the children to equip them for their future. It does not matter how much we invest or provide advantages for our children if we fail to teach them the ways of the Lord. The knowledge of God through the revelation of Christ Jesus is essential. As our children grow up under our tutelage we need to first teach them to be righteous and just. If they learn righteousness and justice they will then do righteousness and justice. The ways of the world produce tyrants and bondage. The ways of the Lord produce peace and freedom. The high ground of any discussion concerning our children's future must include our responsibility to teach them the ways of the Lord, to trust the Lord and to do good.

Sex

> *"There are three things which are too wonderful for me, Four which I do not understand: The way of an eagle in the sky, The way of a serpent on a rock, The way of a ship in the middle of the sea, And the way of a man with a maid."* (Pr 30:18-19 NAS95)

The way of a man with a maid is in many ways still a mystery. The interaction between a man and a woman that leads up to and culminates in what we term "sexual intercourse" is even, in our enlightened age, still shrouded in mystery. Modern science has been able to uncover in great detail the potential outcome of this union that produces the offspring. This ability to procreate and to be instrumental in the development and maturity of our children is in many ways just too wonderful. But for a few moments let us just consider this subject of human sexuality and the morality involved.

For most of the created creatures in this world the purpose of sex is strictly for procreation. In every case sex is an intriguing and often a very involved process. Sometimes it is reliant upon certain conditions or precise timing, driven by a preprogrammed agenda we call instinct. But when we consider human sexuality it takes on added dimensions.

For humans sex becomes more than just a means to procreate, although that is one of its important purposes. The very nature of our human sexuality results in the most intimate of human interactions. It is because we were created in the image and likeness of God that human interaction is much more complex and involved than that of the animal world. We are spiritual beings with complex emotions, desires, intellect, and have the ability to analyze and contemplate ourselves and the world around us. Because of all of this, sex affects us in ways far beyond the fulfillment of physical cravings, and by design was intended to. It was intended that sexual intercourse consummate the union of male and female, joined together to become

unified as one flesh. In the setting of marriage, this most intimate of human interactions, helps to strengthen the bonds of
unity and security.

Most importantly in the discussion about human sexuality is the
fact that God has enabled us as individuals to be in control of our
sexuality. With the ability to control comes the responsibility to
make good choices, for we do not have to allow ourselves to be
controlled by instinct and animal desires. As individuals we are
responsible to consider the ramifications for our actions. We
have no right to override another person's right of choice. This
is the area where choice needs to be protected, before a baby
is conceived, not after.

> **"Marriage [is to be held] in honor among all,**
> **and the [marriage] bed [is to be] undefiled;**
> **for fornicators and adulterers God will judge."**
> (Heb 13:4 NAS95)

There is sacredness in a sexual union that should never be taken
lightly. Outside of marriage sex is cheapened to a level that
only fulfills our physical desires. But we are not merely animals that we should lightly esteem the effects of a union of
male and female, for we are most vulnerable at this juncture
as our nakedness is exposed, physically, emotionally, mentally,
and spiritually. To approach this union from a self-centered perspective ignores these realities and leads to a callousness to
cover the guilt and shame involved with an illicit engagement.

The physical union of a man and a woman has an effect on
them in ways far beyond the physical, and for good reason. For

God intended this union to strengthen and enhance the marriage of male and female, which is the foundation for family. The many industries that have developed around and about sex, both supportive and perverted, attest to the wide-ranging effect it has on us a people. If we were to honestly evaluate the effects of sexual relationships we would have to conclude that healthy relationships need the protection of a marriage commitment. Short-term relationships eventually cause a lot of pain and suffering.

You can only safely hold the high moral ground concerning sexuality if you are in agreement with the Creator regarding sexual relationships. High on the list of considerations is the potential fruit of this relationship, which is our offspring. We are not talking here about simply creating another living organism, but the creation of an eternal soul created in God's image and likeness. This brings a sacredness and sanctity to this union and requires it to be treated with the utmost of respect. In evaluating the sanctity of human life and its eternal value, we cannot simply ignore the moment of its conception and our part in it.

We live at a time and place where our culture is pervaded in every aspect with sexual connotations. Sex is used as a tool for merchants, educators, and politicians. Sex is a gift from God intended to bless mankind, but its perversion becomes a curse in the hands and minds of evil men. The emergence of sex throughout our culture has produced callousness to the ill effects of its misuse. The misuse of sex and its promotion contributes to marital problems, divorce, unwanted children, rape, murder, homosexuality, gender disorders, etc, etc. The list seems to be endless and the effects heartbreaking.

However, none of this changes the reality of the matter. The sacredness of sex is to be preserved in the lifetime commitment of a married couple. Only in this setting can the full blessing of this gift from God be realized. Only within a committed marriage environment can we fulfill our obligation and responsibilities toward a life that is conceived. Only in a committed marriage environment can we abandon ourselves to sexual pleasures and remain safe and secure in the arms of our lover. Only in marriage does this interaction have the approval and blessing of our Heavenly Father.

Divorce

"Yet you say, "For what reason?" Because the LORD has been witness Between you and the wife of your youth, With whom you have dealt treacherously; Yet she is your companion And your wife by covenant. But did He not make [them] one, Having a remnant of the Spirit? And why one? He seeks godly offspring. Therefore take heed to your spirit, And let none deal treacherously with the wife of his youth. "For the LORD God of Israel says That He hates divorce, For it covers one's garment with violence," Says the LORD of hosts. "Therefore take heed to your spirit, That you do not deal treacherously." (Mal 2:14-16 NKJV)

Marriage was the plan of God to join male and female and make them one. Love, caring one for another, was to be the glue that bound them together. The consummation of that love was to result in godly offspring. But what happens when love fails? What happens when one or both partners stop loving? That which was intended to be one becomes fractured and a once peaceful, safe, and loving atmosphere becomes hostile and troubled.

No one wants to live in a hostile and troubled home. The fact is that it did not get to this point overnight. Trouble begins brewing in often little and subtle ways. When we do not address little problems they have a tendency to grow to be big problems. The very nature of marriage and the family that provide a safe environment can also provide an environment that conceals trouble that is brewing. When that trouble erupts it sometimes surprises even those closest to the family. When that hostility erupts, the issues and problems seem insurmountable. Untangling the facts, emotions, and issues seems to be impossible, for simple things become entwined below the surface in complex ways.

Divorce is the simple solution, or so it seems. Divorce promises to allow us to reboot and start over. There actually may be a way to reboot and start over, but divorce is not a part of that solution, and it is not as easy as it sounds. The very fact that a marriage has become a hostile and troubled environment reveals that one or both of these people have not been living according to the standard that God has prescribed, basically loving one another. Having previously discussed what that means we need to focus on a solution for the many of our society that have failed marriages. Divorce is not as good or easy as people have been told it is. Our society as a whole is suffering tremendously because people have bought into the lie that divorce is a solution. The lie declares: if you go your way and I go mine, then everything will be all right.

As with every moral issue, we need to view it from the high moral ground that God has established. From this perspective we can get the best view of the issue and see the best way to address it. If we allow ourselves to be drawn to a lower position we will end up trying to cure a symptom of, rather than the disease (issue) itself. Although each marriage has its unique elements, the fundamentals remain the same for every marriage. Mutual love and respect build a strong marriage, whereas lack of love and hate destroy a marriage.

The high ground is that God hates divorce. God hates it because it is bad for us and He loves us. Marriage is the fundamental structure of a good society and is so by design. Divorce is the dismantling of that structure by undermining the foundation. Family is built upon marriage. Good societies are built upon good families. Good societies produce good nations. Good nations bless the world. Divorce destroys marriage and undermines the family. Likewise, it affects society, the nation, and the world. Divorce is between two people, but it affects many more. Marriage is one of the things that comes from the outflow of love. Divorce comes from the outflow of hate.

> *"He said to them, "Because of your hardness of heart Moses permitted you to divorce your wives; but from the beginning it has not been this way. "And I say to you, whoever divorces his wife, except for immorality, and marries another woman commits adultery."*
> (Mt 19:8-9 NAS95)

Divorce is the exception to the rule. Permission to divorce comes on the heels of blatant immorality and sinful behavior. Divorce is a sentence of judgment, not a solution for healing. The exception for divorce comes because of covenant breaking and unfaithfulness. But in our devolving society any and everything has become an excuse for divorce. Starting with additional reasons for divorce and eventually culminating in no fault divorce, lifelong marriage is now becoming the exception.

As our society is spiraling out of control we need to recognize the huge role that divorce has played in creating this scenario. Divorce creates a chasm that makes repentance and reconciliation very difficult. Marriage and family were built on the rock of righteousness. Love is what was intended to hold it together. In the past, even in societies that had strayed from righteousness, they could be turned toward righteousness in one generation, if family was still foundational. But in today's world these societies are few and far between. Family has been reinvented to be anything or everything. Government is set up to replace God. Right and wrong have become fluid, ever changing at the dictates of an elitist class.

The bottom line is that marriage was founded on the Rock, but the destruction of marriage has left us on shifting sands. It can be argued that divorce is but one of many things that is destroying marriage. But the concept of divorce is a sign or a symbol, of brokenness and unwillingness to reconcile man's will with God's righteousness. It is a replacement of the love connection with the hate divide.

Alternative to Divorce

I know that I have taken a simple divorce, a broken relationship of a man and a woman, and extended it to a national or world problem. But the fact is that every divorce is the destruction of a stone in the foundation of a nation or culture. While divorce was becoming more frequent in America, psychologists, and psychiatrists tried to comfort us by telling us the effects would be minimal and short lived. They were wrong. Every divorce has a far ranging effect that broadens as time goes by. The only real comfort is that the adverse effect can be checked and the long range-effect nullified. Thankfully, there is a God in heaven and He has provided a way of redemption.

For those downstream of divorce, who suffer because of the sins of their parents, God has provided a path of deliverance. It all starts with recognition of the love of a heavenly Father who has provided an invitation to accept adoption into His family. God has provided healing, forgiveness, and adoption through the work of His only begotten Son on the cross. When through repentance people find reconciliation to their Father in heaven, then forgiveness works its way backwards forgiving those who have wronged us. Love and forgiveness can hide a multitude of sins.

The real answer to avoiding the pain and destruction of divorce is to avoid divorce. When a marriage is struggling the couple needs a marriage counselor, not a divorce attorney. Divorce attorneys are not servants of God. Once a couple receives council from a divorce attorney or attorneys, you can almost guarantee that these two people who once pledged their love to each other will walk away hating each other. Most secular marriage counselors will have almost as bad of an effect. It is the council that comes from above that offers true hope and healing. True marriage counseling supports a godly marriage. Love must be restored. Repentance, forgiveness, giving, and receiving are all aspects of the path to reconciliation. This pathway to healing is patterned for us in Scripture. Whereas divorce spreads the seeds of destruction, a healed marriage spreads the seeds of love and peace.

As with arguments on all moral issues, those opposed to God's standards of righteousness will try to lure us down to a lower level to argue their points. We can get wrapped up in the complex details of individual's situations that distract us from the real issues. It is not that there will not be details that need to be dealt with, for there can be complex issues involved. But if we can simply understand the basics of love, marriage, and the destructive nature of divorce, we can then follow and lead people in the direction of righteousness. It is only this pathway that leads to happiness and fulfillment.

Circling Back to the Issue of Abortion

We need to hold to the high moral ground of God's Word on each and every moral issue. But what I have been trying to show is that compromising fundamental principles causes problems that lead up to horrendous decisions. Abortion is murder. But what makes it even worse is that it is murdering the most innocent among us, people who are not guilty of any sin or wrong doing. I have subtly led us on a path to help us understand how we got to the place where people would even consider and seek to justify such evil acts as murdering the unborn.

We have courts that seek to mete out justice to those who violate the law and bring harm to their fellow human beings. But what would be the charge against any of these unborn children if allowed their day in court? Their defense would simply be, "I am innocent." Their question would be, "Why am I condemned to be executed? What is the charge?" If we waited a few years and let these children live, then maybe some of them would eventually do evil, but to condemn them before they even soiled their first diaper seems ludicrous.

In order to reveal the roots of the problem of which abortion is presented as the solution, I brought you back to the beginning. I walked you through creation of family and God's purpose. I walked you through love, marriage, sex, and having children. In each of these areas problems arise when we violate the law of God and its intent to keep us safe, happy, and fulfilled. The problems that arise are the effects of sin.

It is the accumulation of sins and sinful living that finally bring people to the point of accepting the killing of the innocent to cover the sins of the guilty. The acceptance of this as a solution has come about through cunning deception. Legalization and providing convenient abortions do not alleviate the effects. Guilt is increased and a baby is dead. Sacrificing the innocent to hide the sins of the guilty could only be a solution spawned from the pit of hell. The appetite of that pit is never-ending.

God's Solution

As with any problem that has arisen because of sin, the real solution is to start with the root of the problem. I have tried to show that the problem of unwanted children is rooted in rejecting godly living. So let's all just live godly and the problems will go away.

We all know that that is easier said than done. We were not born in the Garden of Eden. We were born in a sinful, sin-scarred world. That is where Jesus comes in. No matter where we are in that pathway of sin that leads to death, there is a way of escape. By the grace of God and the redemptive path Christ has provided, we can escape the path of sin and discover the path that leads to life. The love of God has provided forgiveness and reconciliation that can bring us in right standing with God and can restore proper family relationships. When love becomes the bond that ties us together, then children are the product of love. In this environment there is no fertile ground for Satan's lies and solutions.

CHAPTER 11
Education Ceded to the State

"The Philosophy of the school room in one generation . . . will be the Philosophy of Government in the next." *Abraham Lincoln*

In 1986 Robert Fulghum published a book titled, "All I Really Need to Know I Learned in Kindergarten". As he listed the things that he had learned in kindergarten, the concept of what he was suggesting resonated with many people. The simple fundamentals that were taught in kindergarten were foundational for developing the character of good and loving citizens. I think that it is important to note that Robert Fulghum was born in 1937 and would have entered school in the early 1940's. The godly influence of our founders was still predominating in our public education then. Even our politics was still laced with references from God's Word in those days.

I once read that a child's moral values were established by the time he was eight years old. As a believer in God's Word I do not believe those values are necessarily locked permanently, because God has provided a path of redemption and reconciliation through faith and repentance. Nevertheless we need to understand the importance of early education and its impact on individuals and society. Robert Fulghum was still learning the basics of a civil society in his early education, but subtle changes were already affecting education from early on in the 20th century. Gradually the Christian elements were being weeded out and our historic roots compromised. The concepts of the secular enlightenment and Darwinian Evolution were gaining influence.

Difficult Times Have Come

"But realize this, that in the last days difficult times will come. For men will be lovers of self, lovers of money, boastful, arrogant, revilers, disobedient to parents, ungrateful, unholy, unloving, irreconcilable, malicious gossips, without self-control, brutal, haters of good, treacherous, reckless, conceited, lovers of pleasure rather than lovers of God; holding to a form of godliness, although they have denied its power; and avoid such men as these." (2Ti 3:1-5 NAS)

It was but a few years after Robert was in kindergarten that our schools hosted the children who would play such a role in the turbulent 1960's. These children grew up in an era that promoted family. TV programs like "Father Knows Best" and "Leave it to Beaver" were common. But times were changing and this generation rebelled. What happened, and why did the 60's generation rebel? Had not they learned the same things in kindergarten as Robert Fulghum had? Yet the description of these young people as they approached adulthood would have fit these verses in 2 Timothy.

I think that these young rebels still held to a form of godliness. But their young minds were focused on the hypocrisies around them. They were easily led to find fault with their parents' generation, but yet were too immature to see their own hypocrisy. The majority of these young rebels shouted slogans such as, "Make Love, Not War". But what was lacking in their moral values was what had been eliminated from their education. They had been brought up with basic Christian moral values. But the source and authority of those values had been stripped from their education. The power of Christian morality is in its authority. The power of godliness rests in the authority of the Creator to lead and direct us. When we forget this, our moral values become compromised by selfishness, greed, and self interest.

The 60's revolution altered the course of our nation. This generation sought to correct the hypocrisy and greed around them, but it was an utter failure. It did not correct the materialistic direction in which our country was headed. Many of these idealistic youth slipped back into an even worse course than where their parents were headed. Their children have grown up under an even worse environment. The reason for this is simple. America did not need a new revolution in the 60's. What was needed was a revival; a return to a reverence for the authority of God and His Word. The civilized world is a product of adherence to the law of God. In the measure in which a society adheres to the law of God is the measure in which they experience civilization.

A closer look at the results of the 60's rebellion will show that there was some good that came out of this period. There was limited revival taking place that had a profound effect in the 70's and 80's. There were many that turned to God during this time, and many from these conversions are the voices of reason in our present day and time. Hope was renewed for a time, that America could again be that light on a hill, an example to be followed. But the general direction of our country coming out of the 60's was toward a godless morality that remains in a constant flux of change.

I have digressed into history to show the results of ceding the high ground when it comes to the education of our children. The quote I presented from Abraham Lincoln has proven to be true and the state of our classrooms today prophesies of a dreadful future tomorrow. The only thing that can save us from the anarchy of our future will be a revival. The Trump revival is not enough to save our future. It has been a wakeup call that has alerted some to realize the extreme direction our country is headed. But it has not been enough to bring the majority back to where we need to be morally and spiritually as a country. Each cycle our nation has experienced has ended with our country being a little further from God and our godly roots.

When we are applying the concept of the high moral ground to education we need to realize that our stance needs to be established on different levels. There are godly standards that need to be applied at every level of public education, from pre-school to a PHD. The most important high ground is ceded when we cede our responsibility to educate our children, to the state.

Our Right, Our Responsibility

""And you shall love the LORD your God with all your heart and with all your soul and with all your might. "And these words, which I am commanding you today, shall be on your heart; and you shall teach them diligently to your sons and shall talk of them when you sit in your house and when you walk by the way and when you lie down and when you rise up."
(De 6:5-7 NAS)

"We hold these truths to be self-evident, that all men are created equal, that they are endowed by their Creator with certain unalienable Rights, that among these are Life, Liberty and the pursuit of Happiness." *(Declaration of Independence)*

Let me propose that also among the unalienable rights from God is the right to educate our children. When we are considering rights that are granted to us by our Creator I will also propose that our reception of that right from God comes with a burden of responsibility. No matter which unalienable right we are talking about, each of us must take responsibility for that right if we choose to accept it. As an example: If we have a God-given right to life, then we must choose to live, and take responsibility to feed and nurture that life.

There was only one man who was created fully formed in the likeness and image of God. From him God formed woman.

*"**Male and female created he them; and blessed them, and called their name Adam** (or Man), **in the day when they were created**."* (Ge 5:2 AV) God gave to Man the gift of life and the earth as his inheritance. All of mankind is the product of that gift that was given to Adam, but none of us were fully formed in our humble beginning, nor were we taught directly by God. Each child that is born has the gift of life, but that gift and the responsibility for it was placed in the hands of his parents. There comes a time when that child becomes fully formed, and then the responsibility for his life becomes fully his own. There is a broader discussion that brings in the role of extended family, community, and nation, but I want to focus on the role of the parents and their rights and responsibilities.

From the moment of inception the responsibility of a child's life rests with his parents. The wisdom of God designed a way to provide for life until it becomes fully formed and fully responsible for its own gift of life. That design was family: a father and mother in union. I have already touched on the importance of education emphasizing that the most important aspect of education is what we teach. Now I am emphasizing where the responsibility of that education lies. Adam was educated by God himself. Our children have been preprogrammed to look to us for their education. Primary human instincts and desires all verify the truths taught in Scripture regarding our responsibility to guide and direct our children, and our role to point them to the truth.

Most of our discussions about education focus on schools, vocational training, and exposure to the world around us. In these areas parents do have a vital role and can be instrumental in our children's successes in these areas. I am not suggesting that parents are to be the sole source of a person's education. What I am suggesting is that the responsibility for their education falls on the shoulders of their parents. When parents do not fulfill their responsibility it is ceded to someone else. Not all of those willing to fulfill this responsibility have your child's best interests at heart.

When does a child's education begin? I don't know. But I do know that a child's education begins long before they are born. You may laugh at people who read to their children before they are born. Logically it would seem impossible that the child would understand the words and story line. But we do know that the atmosphere and relationship of those in the household do have an effect on the development of that child. The unborn cannot put their feelings into words, or understand words, but they are learning and experiencing love, or hate, or whatever else is going on. In many ways their identity is being forged even while they are in the womb.

Ceding the high ground on the right and responsibility of parents to educate their own children is one of the most important areas in which the high ground has been ceded. This is one of the important inalienable rights that God has granted us and we have not argued for it from that perspective. I hesitate to say that this is the most important point of my whole book, but it may be. Passing on eternal truth to the next generation is pivotal in determining the outcome of entire people groups for generations into the future. So we need to examine this issue more closely.

"I will give thanks to Thee, for I am fearfully and wonderfully made; Wonderful are Thy works, And my soul knows it very well. My frame was not hidden from Thee, When I was made in secret, And skillfully wrought in the depths of the earth. Thine eyes have seen my unformed substance; And in Thy book they were all written, The days that were ordained for me, When as yet there was not one of them."
(Ps 139:14-16 NAS)

One of the most influential films concerning abortion was "The Silent Scream". Before a baby had the ability to express its feelings it was able to experience pain. We now know that babies are affected by the things his mother consumes. Babies are affected by alcohol, drugs, and cigarette smoke. They do not understand what is happening to them, and they have no means of communicating the discomfort that they feel, but it is very real.

Likewise, there is programmed into each one of us desires that were intended to help us develop and mature to the stature of God's design. Especially in our early development, we do not understand our cravings, know how to fulfill them, or even have the ability to do so. Once we are free of the womb we express our unfilled desires by crying. There are times during this stage of our development that both child and parent experience frustration because of lack of understanding why the baby is crying. When we supply the need of the child (such as feeding them) they become content and the crying stops. If the need was never supplied eventually the crying would become silent and the baby would die.

We all know that babies need more than just milk and can be crying for a lot of different reasons. I have merely used this illustration about milk to point out that the innate desires that we have are there for important reasons and are best fulfilled when we live life as God intended. Modern society has tried to use shortcuts and unnatural means of providing support for our innate desires, but time and again we are confronted with effects of unfulfilled desires. There is more to the benefits of breast feeding than just the milk it provides. It is also true when we provide substitutes for our many desires; they all fall short of God's provision.

Patience, I intend to use all this to help us understand God's plan for education, even though you may be scratching your head wondering where I am taking you. Much of our society has strayed so far from the natural, they can't recognize it when they see it. So I will try to use the natural fulfillment of a baby's desire to parallel our natural desires that lead to the fulfillment that comes through receiving the proper education.

As a baby grows so do his innate desires. We do not usually refer to their exploratory nature as a quest for knowledge, but in a sense it is. Soon after a baby takes its first breath it begins exploring the world around it. To begin with, their world is very small and contained within their limited sight, reach, and hearing. The speed at which their world expands is largely dependent upon those who care for them. The natural inquisitive nature of a child is enhanced by his parents' desire to instill knowledge and understanding. Without the direction and protection of caregivers a child's natural inquisitive nature would probably be the death of him. Often in a person's development their ability to explore exceeds their ability to discern between that which is good or bad, and that which is beneficial or harmful.

Let me wrap all this up by presenting what I think is evidence of the importance of parental education. I think that God has programmed within the parents and the children desires that are only met when the family is functioning properly. When a baby is born, a mother is born. We could spend a great deal of time reviewing the connection a mother has with her children. Even a casual observer can see the incredible bond that develops between a mother and her baby. But even the father is preprogrammed to embrace his children. In our culture we often see fathers distancing themselves from their children, unwilling to accept the responsibility that comes with raising children. But often that resolve is broken down if that father is present at the birth and holds his newborn child. In our present culture where fathers are having a diminishing role in the raising of our children, there still remains within the father an inner craving to connect with their children in a meaningful way.

From my observation there is a God thing going on here. God intended people to provide for their children and there are innate desires that draw them to long for a relationship with their own children. In spite of the fact that our culture is trying to redefine family and relationships, there remains a fierce conflict with our God-given nature that draws us to our children. Just think about all of the things that have been inflicted upon this generation that are at enmity with the God-designed family: sexual perversions, divorce, adultery, feminism, secularism, government interference, etc. Or we could sum it up by just saying sin and selfishness. Yet the unfulfilled relationship between parent and child continues to plague and torture men's souls. My conclusion is that this innate desire was intended to align our children in a position to be educated by their parents.

Likewise, is the desire of children to their parents. I suggest that it is as powerful as the desire of a newborn babe for his mother's breasts. Even much more powerful if you consider how long it lasts and the ramifications if it should be left unfulfilled. In our present culture in which 40% of babies are born out of wedlock, and divorce and dysfunctional families make up much of the remainder, the unfulfilled relationship between father and child has become pronounced. What is it that inspires people to still be searching and inquiring about who their father is, often continuing late into their lives? Is not it the same thing that inspires a six-year-old to say, "I want to grow up to be like my dad"? Is not it the same force that causes people to spend their lives seeking to have their parents' approval? If a person's parents are absent or if their parents do not fulfill the role of mentor and educator, a person is left with a painful longing that seems to be insatiable. Often this desire is not easily understood and rarely articulated clearly. In some ways it becomes another silent scream, a cry not easily expressed, so it is hidden in an aching heart.

> *"And the LORD said, Shall I hide from Abraham*
> *that thing which I do; Seeing that Abraham*

shall surely become a great and mighty nation, and all the nations of the earth shall be blessed in him? For I know him, that he will command his children and his household after him, and they shall keep the way of the LORD, to do justice and judgment; that the LORD may bring upon Abraham that which he hath spoken of him." (Ge 18:17-19 AV)

Every innate desire created in us was for a purpose in God's plan. God's plan was that we would raise up our children in the ways of the Lord, to do justice and judgment. That intense desire for the one on one relationship between parent and child was for this purpose. Somehow, in spite of the testimony of our innate desire and the admonition of God throughout His Word we have ignored this right and responsibility parents have to their children and children have to their parents. Deceptive voices have lured us to lower levels and convinced us that our duties were fulfilled simply by assuring that our children were educated. The important thing is WHAT we are taught, not that we are taught. And being taught the right thing is enhanced when it comes from our parents.

Ceding this high ground in our discussions and actions has allowed the enemy to virtually kidnap most of an entire generation of children. It has resulted in the transformation of our culture before our very eyes. Our Christian culture has become a pagan culture while we hopelessly stand by and wonder how and why this came to be. Much of it can be attributed to this one issue in which the high ground was ceded and we allowed the enemy to educate our children. Just as in the movie, "The

Silent Scream", we have seen the writhing action of children in disobedience, oblivious to the cause of their discomfort and in essence their silent scream, their cry for a meaningful relationship with their parents.

CHAPTER 12
Our Identity

Who Am I?

"for if you are living according to the flesh, you must die; but if by the Spirit you are putting to death the deeds of the body, you will live. For all who are being led by the Spirit of God, these are sons of God. For you have not received a spirit of slavery leading to fear again, but you have received a spirit of adoption as sons by which we cry out, "Abba! Father!" The Spirit Himself bears witness with our spirit that we are children of God," (Ro 8:13-16 NAS)

I have spent a considerable amount of time emphasizing the importance of parental involvement in a child's education. I also tried to show how our innate natural desires were designed to bring parents and children together for that purpose. Let me remind you that I am assuming that I am speaking to godly parents who are instructing their children in the ways of the Lord, because it is the content of our instruction that is essential in understanding my next point.

A good education is valuable on many different levels. It gives us a lens in which we view the world. It prepares us for developing job skills, a means of providing a living. It gives us communication skills. It helps us build relationships with people. But of all the things we could list, none would stand out as much as what it can mean in establishing our identity.

The innate desire of children toward their parents is so very valuable in providing a platform for parents to teach their children. But the root of that desire is the need to establish their individual identity. That is why the conduct and character of the parents is so important. To start with, it is natural for children to identify with their parents. But as children become increasingly aware of the world around them it is important that the object of their inspiration is desirable. It is of most importance that the parents reflect the model that their child should follow.

We all know that there will come times in a child's life when the natural inclination toward their parents will be challenged. Since our culture is being transformed from a Christian culture to a pagan culture, the diversity outside of the Christian home presents a multitude of questions and challenges for any child. Two forces are working upon your child; the culture and peer pressure. As a small child in a loving Christian home a child's identity was secure and comfortable. But outside of the home and during this time of growth a child is vulnerable to the forces that would lure him in an attempt to capture his identity. Conflicting struggles within him, desiring to be unique and at the same time to be like others, can add to the conflict.

Those who have grown up in dysfunctional families, and those who have been deprived of one or both parents offer insight into the major issue at stake here. That issue is one of identity, or who we are and of what significance is our life. Identifying with our peers, and flowing with the culture, in the end leaves a person empty and unfulfilled. That longing for identity with family seems to intensify and become more obvious and distinct in those who have never known their own parents. The strength of desire compels some to diligently seek to discover who their parents are. For others it may be unresolved relationships that plague them. In spite of the odds that predict a search for absent parents will end in disappointment, many people have persisted in their quest. Why? I think the reason is because many people have unresolved identity issues. I think every one of us would have to admit that rooted in each of us is a desire to belong, to find our own identity of where we come from and where we belong.

I have stressed the importance of that early connection with our parents and their responsible role in our education. That early connection can satisfy those early cravings for identity and set a child on the path to find fulfillment of their destiny. When that early connection is disrupted the child becomes vulnerable as they aimlessly wander, seeking to understand who they are and what is the purpose of life. The rate of suicide, juvenile delinquency, and their link to the decay of the family structure is testimony of this fact.

But getting started on the right path is only the beginning. As our culture drifts from its Biblical roots the environment is becoming increasingly hostile toward Christianity. Even the institutions that were created to support Christianity have in many cases become compromised in this environment. In an attempt to satisfy their critics, many have opted to cut themselves off from

Christianity's roots, not realizing that this jeopardizes their end. This environment is challenging even for those who had the advantage of a good start in life. What then is the hope of those who did not have a good start in life? There remains hope for all and that hope lies in the testimony of those who have held to the high moral ground and steadfastly held to their identity.

Just as a child instinctively finds their identity in their parents, good parental education leads that child in an understanding of Man's relationship with God. The goal is for our child to establish an identity with our Creator and His plan and purpose. In the beginning of a child's life he can find identity with Christ through his identity with his parents. But as time goes on he must establish that identity apart from his parents. If we neglect the revelation given to us in those early chapters of Genesis, and fail to teach it, we can leave people with the illusion that their identity with Christ can be established through our earthly parents. The attack on those early chapters of the Bible, whether through so-called science or modern theology, are for the purpose of convincing people that our identity with God can be achieved in different ways.

Our innermost desires cannot be fulfilled until we find our identity in God, our Creator. The opening chapters of the Bible reveal to us the reason why our natural identity was compromised when man sinned, identifying us with the rebellion. But also, even in those early chapters we are given hope and a promise. That promise came to fruition through our Lord and Savior Jesus the Christ. Jesus, the sinless Son of Man and Son of God, has restored man's identity with his Creator. Because of this we can through Christ restore our identity with God. Jesus not only provided a way for us, but he also showed us the way. "You must be born again."

> *"For both He who sanctifies and those who are sanctified are all from one Father; for which reason He is not ashamed to call them brethren,"* (Heb 2:11 NAS)

Whether our discussions are about science, politics, theology, or whatever, people may try to identify us with a thought or an idea. A description of our understanding in any of these areas may be termed conservative, liberal or whatever, but as Christians we need to establish our identity in Christ and not in our present understanding. If we do this, we position ourselves in an attitude that is easily molded into the image of Christ as we grow in the grace and knowledge of the Lord.

We are established on the high moral ground by our identity as a child of God. To argue any point from a position as a conservative, or republican, or even an American, is to cede that high moral ground that is found only in Christ. It is not that our stances will not be conservative, or that we will not be liberal in our graciousness, or that we will not support our Country's godly roots, but the reasons for our convictions ought to find roots in our identity as a child of God and our standing in Christ Jesus.

> *"Which was the son of Enos, which was the son of Seth, which was the son of Adam, which was the son of God."* (Lu 3:38 AV)

What I have been trying to show you is that even now there lies within each of us the longing to identify as a child of God, belonging to God Himself. Even though separated by sin, there lies within each of us, that innate desire that can only be satisfied by reconnecting to our Heavenly Father. When that connection takes place we find our identity and sense of belonging. Adam was a son of God. Now we also can become sons of God through Christ Jesus.

Once we find our identity as a child of God through Christ Jesus, that identity takes central stage and defines who we are. From this position everything gains a new perspective. As the Apostle Paul stated *"Therefore if any man be in Christ, he is a new creature: old things are passed away; behold, all things are become new."* (2Co 5:17 AV)

> *"The Spirit itself beareth witness with our spirit, that we are the children of God:"* (Ro 8:16 AV)

Our Christian Identity

I feel the need to clarify our Christian identity. Simply put, it is the identity that is found in Christ as a child of God. Within and without Christianity there has been compromised and misleading information that has led to confusion as to what a true Christian identity is. I will attempt to provide a basic understanding, realizing that there are heights and depths of this that would fill volumes. The entire Bible is a revelation of who Christ is and His plan of redemption.

First, let me define who Jesus Christ is. He is the only begotten Son of God, the manifestation of God in the flesh. He is the Word made flesh, the revelation of God. Through Him all things were created and all things were created for Him. Through Him we are reconciled to God through His death on the cross. In other words, through Him, and Him only, can we find our identity as a son of God. He came into this world and lived as a man. His life and teachings reveal to us the very heart of God and His love for us. He was the sacrifice for our sins and suffered a sinner's death on the cross as a substitute for us. Through His resurrection He conquered death, hell, and the grave, verifying His promise of life everlasting to all that believe on Him. He is Lord and Savior of all that trust in Him.

A Christian is a follower of Christ. A Christian is one who has followed Christ in death and resurrection. Water baptism is a testimony of a Christian's death and resurrection. A Christian is a person who has received the promise of salvation through Jesus Christ. He has been born again by the Spirit of God, a new creation in Christ, delivered from the bondage of sin.

The path of salvation is revealed in Scripture. A person who believes the message of Jesus Christ puts their faith in Christ Jesus to save them. They acknowledge their sin and repent, turning from their sinfulness and following the teachings of Jesus, making Jesus Lord of their life. In obedience they follow Christ in water baptism and receive the promise of the Father, the indwelling Spirit of God. It is the spiritual seed that is planted by God's Holy Spirit that makes them a child of God. In a nutshell a Christian is a disciple of Jesus Christ. A Christian's confession is that Jesus Christ is Lord and they live their life in accord with that confession. It is through Christ that we at last truly find our identity as a child of our Creator, our Father in heaven.

Finding our identity as a child of God fulfills that innate desire that has driven us from birth. We now truly know who we are and have peace. But this is just the beginning of our journey. We soon realize that there is much more to learn as we begin our eternal journey. Just as a newborn baby our understanding of our world will continue to grow and mature in our faith and walk with our Lord.

> *"And we know that God causes all things to work together for good to those who love God, to those who are called according to His purpose. For whom He foreknew, He also predestined to become conformed to the image of His Son, that He might be the first-born among many brethren;"* (Ro 8:28-29 NAS)

The opportunity to be reconciled to God is the heart of the Gospel. Establishing our identity as a child of God is the answer to our deepest longings. Once established it becomes foundational to who we are becoming. You may recognize that this is where we arrive on the moral high ground, for here we are in harmony with God and His Law.

Keep in mind also that we are all individuals. Just as God is more than just our Creator and has many descriptive names, so we also have differing attributes that are part of our identity, or who we are. I am also a man, husband, father, friend, farmer, introvert, scholar, etc.. Each one of us has a different list and that list changes with time. What is most important in the keeping of who we are is prioritizing our own identity. The high ground slopes off real quick when we get our priorities mixed up.

We must be first and foremost a Christian. No matter what else is on our list it should be preceded by our identity as a child of God. For instance: if I am a husband, I need to be a Christian husband. Each and every thing that is part of our identity should be preceded with our Christian identity. I am emphasizing this because we are encouraged in our present culture to relegate our Christian identity. We cannot allow this to happen, because if we do we endanger our identity. If we allow anything to trump our identity in Christ we become guilty of idolatry. If we do not repent of this sin, we will eventually lose our standing as a child of God.

If we first acknowledge Christ as Lord, then the rest of the list of who we are will be arranged in the proper order of priority. But if we fail to identify first as a follower of Christ, then we begin this slippery slope that ends with our loss of identity. This is true with an individual, a church, or a nation. There are many people, churches, and our own nation that has lost or is losing their identity and often are Christian in name only. Hold to the High Ground!

> *"By this we know that we love the children of God, when we love God and observe His commandments."* (1Jo 5:2 NAS)

Race and Racism

"Now the man called his wife's name Eve, because she was the mother of all the living."
(Ge 3:20 NAS)

In this year of 2019 in the United States of America racism has become a major topic, and to be accused of racism seems to have risen to the top of the list of unpardonable sins. The irony of this scenario is that those who are wielding this accusation as a club are some of those most guilty of this charge. Racism is indeed a grievous sin. Racism has often raised its ugly head throughout the history of mankind. Even within the organized Church it has at times been present and sometimes even prevalent. But it is only in the message that was commissioned to the Church that the cure for this infectious sin can be found. It is probably because much of the organized Church has avoided dealing with this issue that it has now become a tool in the promotion of a godless culture. This is another one of those areas where Christianity has suffered loss because they surrendered the high moral ground on this issue.

First, we need to define the term race so we know what we are talking about. I will use the "Merriam-Webster" kid's definition, to keep things simple.

Race: (1) any one of the groups that human beings can be divided into based on shared distinctive physical traits (2) a group of individuals who share a common culture or history **//** the English *race* (3) a major group of living things **//** the human *race*

Racial discrimination is as old as the hills. It has been with us as far as we have recorded history. People by nature usually prefer and favor those who are like them or have a shared culture or history. One of the most defining features that has segregated people is that of language. If we all spoke the same language it would be a lot easier to understand those who have a different history and culture than our own.

History of Race

Separated by language, geography, and separate histories, it is no wonder that time has produced a great diversity of cultures. The intersection of cultures often produced either trade or war and those interactions could create more or less diversity. Kings, nations, and empires rise and fall but man's desire for security and identity remain. That innate desire for identity that we focused on in our last section is a driving force that can unite us or divide us. One thing we need to keep in mind is that diversity of language and distinguished nations was God's idea. We will not discuss the reason and purpose of these divisions here, but God's idea of nations was not for the intention of elevating or devaluing our various characteristic differences.

A brief history of our racial distinctions in America may help us understand the root of our present problem here in the United States. In the early 1800's an American physician and natural scientist, Samuel Morton, categorized humans by their prominent features. By measuring the capacity of skulls from different people groups (assuming that greater capacity equaled greater intelligence) Morton determined that there were five races of people. Listing them in order of supposed intelligence they were Caucasians, East Asians, Southeast Asians, American Indians, and Negros. Morton hypothesized that there had been five separate creations in which God positioned them in separate homelands. Morton's theories were very popular in his day. His followers, Josiah C. Nott and George Gliddon, made a monumental tribute to Morton's theories by publishing "Types of Mankind" in 1854. The discussions that followed took a dramatic turn after Charles Darwin published his manuscript, "On the Origin of Species by Means of Natural Selection, or the Preservation of Favored Races in the Struggle for Life", just a few years later.

Just because a belief becomes popular does not make it true. And just because something is true is no guarantee it will become popular. Theories like Morton's and Darwin's become popular because people wanted them to be true. In a world that had tolerated slavery for centuries, these theories resonated with people desiring to justify their beliefs and actions. I have lived long enough to realize that there is nothing that cannot be rationalized. People work hard at justifying their behavior. It is amazing how even the Scriptures can be twisted to undermine the clear reading of God's Holy Word. The secret to personal justification is to start with your theory (what you desire to be true) and pick and choose those facts that fit into your predetermined outcome.

But then there is the unadulterated Word of God. Those who put their trust in the Scripture hold to the high moral ground on the issue of race. As was stated in Genesis 3:20, the first woman was named Eve because she was the mother of all humans. There never was more than one race. We are all of one blood, offspring of Adam and Eve, the parents of the human race. And most important to note is that we were all created in the image and likeness of God Himself. This is the reason that all people have intrinsic value. It is confidence in this revelation in Scripture that has inspired the fulfillment of Christ's commission of the Church to preach the Gospel to every tribe and nation. It is this truth that makes it possible for every soul to be reconciled to God and become an inheritor in the Kingdom of God.

People throughout history who have put their trust in the Word of God have found it to be true. Those who have been willing to look beyond the superficial difference have found within all people groups that kindred spirit that makes us human. This spiritual connection we all have is evidence of the truthfulness of God's Word. But for those who are not willing to go beyond the superficial, there is revelation that is taking place through the science of our day that confirms God's claim of the kinship of all people. The ongoing research of DNA is affirming that all people are descendents of one man and one woman. DNA research is also teaching us about our differences. Things like skin color and facial features are minor differences. Often there are greater differences between people of the same skin color than there are between people who have great differences in skin color. My point is that God's Word was correct and is worthy of our trust. The way in which we view our ethnic differences is best seen through the lens of God's Word.

So my question for those of faith is: why is the secular left leading the discussion about race when we have the high moral ground here? The answer of course is because some have ceded the high moral ground and have been lured to a lower level in our discussions concerning race.

> *"And hath made of one blood all nations of men*
> *for to dwell on all the face of the earth, and hath*
> *determined the times before appointed, and*
> *the bounds of their habitation;"* (Ac 17:26 AV)

What then is the answer to racism, the discrimination or favor of one people group over another? For those who trust God's wisdom, it is the acknowledgment of the truth that we are all of one family, and we are to treat each other as we would like to be treated. This principle was articulated in our foundational documents and was once the basis of our public education. Basically, if we were to just follow the spirit of our foundational law it would work toward eliminating racial inequality through our courtrooms and our classrooms. Eliminating discrimination from the human heart is a more difficult matter. Much that has been accomplished through the courts and the classroom in the past is now being overturned in both places. It is the departure from our godly roots that has at many times slowed the process of reducing racism.

It is important that we understand the adverse effect that has resulted from allowing the secular left to dominate the conversation concerning racism. Although their claimed agenda is to combat racism, the opposite is true. While they accuse others of racism, they themselves promote it. All of the gains that had been accomplished in this country over the last 200 years are in jeopardy of being lost by their promotion of race. The dream of Martin Luther King Jr. that his children would be judged by their character and not their skin color is in jeopardy. It seems that in every field whether it be history, science, the arts, music, theater, media, politics, law enforcement, criminal justice, language, or whatever, the secular left tries to focus our attention away from the issue and onto race.

I spent a good deal of time showing how important identity is to us. Reestablishing our identity as a child of God is of utmost importance in establishing our relations to each other. To harbor pride or distain simply because of skin color or ethnicity is a sin against God and humanity. If we were to focus rather on truth and justice then it would reveal those who are guilty of this sin. Race is a false narrative, but a great tool to divide people and undermine truth and justice.

To illustrate my point let's take a snapshot out of history from the 1400's. Europe was occupied mostly by Caucasians. China was populated by East Asians. Africa was populated with black-skinned people. And the Americas were populated by reddish brown-skinned people. In which of these areas did peace and justice reign? Peace and justice were eluded and in all of these arenas, conflict reigned. Obviously they did not need racial tensions to fuel hatred, discrimination, violence, and injustice. But what did help to civilize the world and cause people to respect each other? In every one of these arenas it was the Gospel of Jesus Christ that was the one factor that worked in bringing about peace and justice.

Before I leave this discussion of maintaining the high moral ground in respect to racism, I feel like I need to address the attempts to bring peace and justice without using the authority of God's Word. I am not ignorant of those who do address these issues from the perspective of the "brotherhood of man". Science has produced a tremendous amount of evidence that we indeed are all descendents of one man and one woman. But my experience has taught me that the issue of race is much deeper than simply people's intellect. One of the great hurdles in combating racism is rooted in history, both true history and false history. For many people it can be a personal history, the things they have experienced. It is these histories that are used as justification to combat hatred with hatred. The results entrench racism rather that reduce it.

That is why the Biblical record is so important. Not only are we taught that we all are family, members of Adam's race, but we are given the history or sin and its effects. Reestablishing our identity as children of God came at the cost of Christ's sacrifice on the cross. The bottom line is, that for us to overcome our histories, a whole lot of forgiveness had to be accomplished. The cost of forgiveness is paid by the victims; in this case it was Jesus who paid the price for us. Because He forgave we also can have the power to forgive. We need to remember that the big sin of racism is a sin against God.

God is not a respecter of persons and neither should we be. In other words, there is no room for racism in the Kingdom of God. Our laws in America reflect this principle even though it is not always reflected in individual's actions. If we want to eliminate racial preference and discrimination in our country we must first uphold the law. Secondly, we must stop referring to people as belonging to different races. Thirdly, we need to recognize that we cannot change the past. The sins of past generations are never justification of the sins of a present generation. If we are to see racism disappear in the future, we have to deal with it in the present. We cannot fix past sins and are foolish if we think we can bear the burden of the sins of the past or find restitution for the offenses of the past.

I realize that my simple suggestions for combating racism would need to be more fully explained to be understood by many people. It was not my intention to even delve this deep into it when I began writing. I merely wanted to show how very important it is that we do not give up the high moral ground on this subject. Simply put, we are all of one blood (descendents of Adam and Eve) and were created in the image and likeness of God. Racism is a sin against God and man, violating the Law of God that we love our neighbor as we love ourselves.

It's About Our Identity

If there was anyplace that has had an opportunity to eliminate racism it was here in America. But it seems that the opportunity is slipping by us. It is not because ethnicity is not part of our identity, because it is part of who we are. But if we start from the top and work our way down we will discover that finding our identity in Christ sets everything in order. We have to start our list from the foundational level and work our way up, because what we are foundationally will reflect in every aspect of who we appear to be.

I will use myself as an example of how we should define ourselves. First I am Christian (a child of God), a husband, father, son, a Gunderson, a citizen of a Christian nation (United States),

Norwegian and German heritage, etc. etc. To fully describe who I am would include a long list of things including what occupations I have had, what I like, and what I have done. The most important thing is that I am first a son of God. Everything else down the list cannot be understood without this knowledge. I am a Christian husband and a Christian father. Because Christian has become foundational to who I am, it changes every aspect of my identity. I have more in common with a Christian from an African heritage than I do with a person who is an atheist from an American or Norwegian heritage. My perspective of different people groups (no matter how you group them) is determined by the perspective of my heavenly Father. My identity and kinship is with the sons of God (Christians); this is my family. But my ethnicity stems from the rebellious sons of Adam that have not yet been redeemed. My desire is that they too would be freed from the bondage to sin, be reconciled to God, and be able to identify with me as a son of God.

Even our American citizenship should trump our ethnic identity. The foundational law of this nation sets every citizen on equal standing. Our Declaration of Independence acknowledged that all men were created equal. Any form of racism is a violation of this declaration. This is not to say that there are not benefits to being an American citizen, just as there are benefits that come with becoming a son of God. These benefits are not based upon our ethnicity, but are based upon our fulfillment of the requirements to becoming a citizen.

CHAPTER 13
Lost Identity

___

W hat happens with a loss of identity and where does it lead? Sin fractured our identity, alienating us from God. Likewise, many in our present culture have fractured family ties, leaving them alienated from their family and paternal identity. Presently our nation is experiencing ideological divisions and a transformation from being a Christian nation to pagan nation, causing many to lose their national or American identity. Rejection of truth has also resulted in some even losing their gender identity. These are all root identities that are fundamental in our existence. When they are fractured people begin looking elsewhere hoping to find something to provide a connection for them. Our innate desire for identity cries out to be satisfied.

As I have already stated, nothing is going to satisfy our desire for identity like reconciliation with God would do for us. If we can be reconciled with our Father in heaven it will provide emotional, mental and spiritual healing. Even if we never establish our identity with our earthly family, or a national identity, we can be made whole because God will provide that family and kingdom identity for us. But without God, when there is a loss of family and a national or ethnic identity, the desire for a personal identity becomes intense. That craving in turn creates vulnerability for people to be taken advantage of, and no one knows this better than the enemy of our souls.

Independence

"Independent and free" were once presented as being synonymous with being an American citizen. For the founders of the colonies and later the United States, this meant that we were free to govern ourselves within Biblical moral standards. Each individual was free to pursue the potential of his God-given life within the bounds of those standards. Equality under the law for everyone provided the security of those individual freedoms of our God-endowed rights. If you think about it, I am sure you can see how that this freedom was intended to allow us to find our true identity. As I have pointed out, that identity is rooted in heavenly Father. In God's eyes we are equal in value but as unique as our fingerprints. In other words, the development of our identity will not be the same as anyone else's.

The removal of God and His Law has created an entirely different concept of independence and freedom for our present generation. Our country, which was once referred to as a land of opportunity, has now become a land where you can receive your desires at the expense of someone else. Equality has been shifted from opportunity to outcome. This goal is unattainable, but the pursuit of it will result in the total loss of freedom for everyone. The independence proposed is an independence from God. The freedom to do as one pleases is a freedom from God's law that is intended to protect us. The bondage that results is a bondage to sin and tyrants.

Creating Your Own Identity

"And which of you by worrying can add a single hour to his life's span?" (Lu 12:25 NAS95)

It is in this environment that the subtle twist on freedom is presented in this phrase: "You can be anything you want to be." This may sound good and seem like an inspirational message to give to our children, but is it true? Freedom from kings and dictators was intended to keep others from forcing us into a mold of their choosing. But when we deny that we were intended to find our identity as a child of God, we set the course for an attempt to create our own identity, and the ramifications for that are seen in the resulting failures and perversions.

"Under three things the earth quakes, And under four, it cannot bear up: Under a slave when he becomes king, And a fool when he is satisfied with food, Under an unloved woman when she gets a husband, And a maidservant when she supplants her mistress." (Pr 30:21-23 NAS)

Our identity begins with a DNA blueprint and a God-given gift of life. It has been said that we all are a product of our heredity and our environment. This simplistic explanation leaves out some important factors; the most import one is that of choice. We all are confronted with the revelation of God in various ways, both subtle and dramatic. When we choose to pursue our God-given identity in Him, then our journey is one of discovery and application. We are in discovery of our inherent potential, and of finding application to the time and place in which we live. Of all generations we are most privileged in having the revealed Word of God so readily available to guide us in this journey. Our choices play a large role in who we become, but our original blueprint remains foundational. Trusting God to help us develop that unique blueprint will be a constant comfort and inspiration. It is in our God-given identity that we find meaning and purpose.

But if we turn from the revelation of God, denying that life is found in Him, we are left to seek our identity elsewhere. It all begins with a denial of the image and likeness in which we are fashioned. It is not that we are not granted a broad spectrum of choices, but the reality is that those choices are limited within the scope of who we were created to be. When Eve was told she could be like God, it was a lie. If someone had told me as a child I could be seven feet tall if I really wanted to be, it would have been false. The lie of the devil is that you can be whatever you want to be; you can create your own identity. The truth is, that each one of us has a unique root identity on which to build. When we build on it within the safety of God's laws our life has meaning and purpose.

> *"For the wrath of God is revealed from heaven*
> *against all ungodliness and unrighteousness of*
> *men, who suppress the truth in unrighteousness,*
> *because that which is known about God is*
> *evident within them; for God made it evident*
> *to them. For since the creation of the world*
> *His invisible attributes, His eternal power and*
> *divine nature, have been clearly seen, being*
> *understood through what has been made,*

so that they are without excuse. For even though they knew God, they did not honor Him as God, or give thanks; but they became futile in their speculations, and their foolish heart was darkened. Professing to be wise, they became fools, and exchanged the glory of the incorruptible God for an image in the form of corruptible man and of birds and four-footed animals and crawling creatures." (Ro 1:18-23 NAS)

A denial of the truth produces fools and foolish speculation, exchanging the glory of God for corruption.

"Therefore God gave them over in the lusts of their hearts to impurity, that their bodies might be dishonored among them. For they exchanged the truth of God for a lie, and worshiped and served the creature rather than the Creator, who is blessed forever. Amen. For this reason God gave them over to degrading passions; for their women exchanged the natural function for that which is unnatural, and in the same way also the men abandoned the natural function of the woman and burned in their desire toward one another, men with men committing indecent acts and receiving in their own persons the due penalty of their error. And just as they did not see fit to acknowledge God any longer, God gave them over to a

***depraved mind, to do those things which are
not proper,"*** (Ro 1:24-28 NAS)

I have already touched on some of the issues that have arisen
as man has distanced himself from his Creator. My focus here
is to show how following a godless path leads people to eventually seek to be their own creator, as foolish as this sounds.
People have flipped reality. Instead of accepting that we have
descended from God, they assert that we can ascend to be God.

I have already spent some time dealing with sex and its proper
role. But those things that were once of such a personal nature
that they were kept behind closed doors have now become
center stage. The beauty of God's design and interaction of the
separate genders has been marred by many perverted acts that
violate the sanctity of this relationship. But when it is done correctly the relationship between man and woman provides comfort, safety, companionship, and the avenue through which new
life enters the world. In addition to these things, it is obvious
that God intended the union of man and woman to help to
forge our identity. Marriage unites male and female together in
a unit God calls, Man. When I married my wife we became, Mr.
and Mrs. Gunderson, or Bob and Rachel, for those who knew
us best. Each of us is the result of the consummation of male
and female. It is who we are, and the further we drift from the
truth the greater our identity crisis becomes.

I am reminding you of some basics to explain the departure
from reality that our society is pursuing. How did we get to a
place where individuals seek to identify themselves as something they are not? How did a society get to the place that they

would support the idea that a man could identify as a woman or vice versa? How can a society advanced in science and logic entertain the concept that a person's imagined identity should trump their physical reality?

I believe what we are seeing in our culture today is the result of people's quest to fulfill their desire for identity in a world that has distanced itself from God. If you have followed me this far you have seen how important it is to establish our identity. It is an innate desire that reveals itself in different ways. The purpose of this desire is that we seek to connect with our Father in heaven. We can see in our relationship with our earthly father and mother how God leads us toward Himself. We can also see how, when we are deprived of our mother and father, people seek their identity in their association with an idol, a gang, friends, peers, or whatever or whoever. The problem with these avenues is that they never fully satisfy our basic need for identity.

With the breakdown of family and culture there is an open door for everything from cults to political organizations to take priority in defining a person's identity. Normally there are a range of things that define who we are as a person. We seek not only to find and establish our own identity, but also acceptance within that identity. It is not only our core identity but the affirmation of that identity that seems to be necessary to satisfy this basic need. The bottom line is that none of our affiliations are going to satisfy our basic desire for the affirmation of our identity.

This brings us to the issue of LGBT and why it has become an identity issue. The categories represented by these letters represent deviant sexual behaviors, and have been around for a long time. These behavior problems were addressed in the Scripture and condemned because they violate the precepts of God that were intended to keep us safe. As a society drifts further from God these types of behaviors become more common and as such affect a broader segment of society. As we progressed in the understanding of our physical world, our knowledge of the damage these behaviors had on the people's physical, mental, and social lives became evident. In an effort to distance themselves from the clear mandates of Scripture, our intellectuals referred to these actions as being the result of mental disorders or illnesses. From there it was a slippery slope to finally arrive where we are today. Our societal view went from sin, to sickness, to misunderstood and oppressed, and finally arriving at acceptance as a natural state of being worthy of celebration.

As our society was sliding in this direction there were many who were unconcerned, even in the Christian community. Their attitude was that the actions of others did not affect them and so it did not matter. But as these unnatural behaviors were moved from the behavior category to the identity category they ended up center stage. A generation estranged from their connection to God, family, history, and culture, is seeking for an identity. For some their letter L, G, B, or T became their identity, or who claimed to be. But assuming an identity based upon their sexual behavior was not enough. There remained within them an intense desire for affirmation.

Pandora's Box has been opened and there seems to be no end in sight. People are grasping at anything and everything in an attempt to define their identity. It is indeed a world turned up-side-down. America did not get this way overnight. But what has happened to America in my lifetime has been shocking. The speed of our transformation continues to escalate. At the heart of the matter is our identity, our personal identity as well as our identity as a nation. Who and what we identify with is crucial to who we are and what we will become. How do we as Christians address this identity crisis?

We cannot give up the high moral ground here or it will be an endless battle. We can see how the deterioration of our culture has left many people drifting without an anchor. Having an identity is crucial for our well-being. We can see the many ways people seek to find their own identity and how those avenues often fail to satisfy our innate desire. We have seen how in desperation people have come to seek their identity in behavior when the normal associations fail them. It is our identity as Christians that we need to exhibit by example and testimony, for this is the answer for the healing of these desperate souls.

Marring the Physical Image

We can see how that the silent scream and pain of lost identity have affected people's actions in their quest to create their own identity. It is not enough for people to just have an identity, but they also crave affirmation from others. Gender identity is not a new phenomenon. Gender is an important part of our Christian identity. Marriage brings the two into a common identity. The loss of a Christian identity creates an insecurity that is often acted out as men and women try to impress others of their masculinity or femininity. Without Godly morality those actions include sex outside of the safe bonds of marriage. Romans 1 exposes the degradation and abuse of people's bodies that results from following a path of rebellion to God and where it leads.

Solomon said that there was nothing new under the sun. Sexual perversion is not a new phenomenon. But the loss of shame in my lifetime in America seems to have brought us to new lows. Those sins that were once hidden for shame, are now blatantly exhibited. We have digressed from marriage to sexual freedom, to homosexuality, to same sex-marriage, to cross-dressing, to identifying as the opposite sex, and finally surgically and chemically deforming bodies to resemble the opposite sex. I cringe thinking where this will all end.

A generation of lost identities elevates and parades these deviant behaviors. Shamelessly they proclaim their pride in sin and choose it as their identity. Blatantly they demand that we all affirm their new created identities, no matter how distorted and absent they are from reality. And a country without a moral compass meets their demands.

The Nation's Identity

As our country is attempting to convert our culture and nation from a Christian nation into a secular one, a new identity must be forged. The very root of that new identity is what will eventually destroy the emerging society. Whereas our nation was built upon the principle that all men are created equal, the emerging society is based upon the principles of evolution. Our freedom has been experienced by the measure in which our laws and culture reflected our founding principles. It was the acceptance of the laws of our Creator that preserved that freedom. Envy and pride are two forces that undermine that freedom by inspiring lawless behavior. It is this abuse of freedom that has fueled the illusions that freedom can exist in a secular society. For when the concept of our universal identity as God's creation is totally erased, then our freedom will also cease to exist.

The root of our new secular identity is evolution. In other words, everything made itself. As the pinnacle of this mindless, purposeless process of evolution, mankind is becoming "god". We have "evolved" to the point where we are solely in control of our own destiny. From this "progressive" mindset nothing is sacred because everything is evolving. Truth for the "progressives" is relative. In their imaginative world anything can be true, so therefore nothing is true. "Progressive" is the term the godless use to identify themselves. Rejecting the timeless truths or their Creator it is only in their imagination that their ever-changing standards could be considered "progressive".

The irony is, that outside of the environment that was created by those who built this culture and nation, their world would collapse. Their imaginary world in which moral values are continually in flux creates uncertainty and chaos. In their "progressive" mindset they propose that they can take a society built upon the absolute laws of science and truth and operate it under the assumption that their wishes and desires can be fulfilled simply by declaring them to be so.

The "progressives" have been able to propel us as people and a nation to the point that we are existing on deficit spending. The wealth that was created through hard work and sacrifice is being squandered. Just like the prodigal son squandered his inheritance in riotous living, this nation will eventually come to their senses when their wealth is gone and they are destitute.

Instead of cherishing our heritage, our nation is becoming bankrupt financially and morally. Through fiscal irresponsibility deficit spending will eventually bankrupt a country. In the same way, irresponsibly ignoring the laws of God will eventually bring a nation to moral bankruptcy. Since the Christian moral values the country was founded on are no longer taught in our institutes of learning, morality is in flux. The protections afforded by godly moral standards are diminishing as the older generations are passing away. Without a godly standard, moral bankruptcy is inevitable.

The Church's Identity

Without God, we as individuals lose our true identity. Without Christ, the Church also loses its identity. The Church was intended to be the body of Christ here on earth. The head of that body is Christ. Churches, like people can end up being Christian in name only. The moral high ground remains unwavering and unchanging. When Churches cede the high ground they end up in a compromised position and their identity as the body of Christ is lost. In regards to the subject of identity, the Church has a responsible role to play. The Church is to uphold the standard that has come from heaven, which is God's Word. The Church is to be a moral compass reliably pointing to righteousness and truth. As a compass it is intended to point people to the path to establishing their identity with God their Father. Another important role of the Church is to provide affirmation of our identity through ministering the Word and the bond of love and fellowship found in the family of God.

When the Church cedes the high ground the compass become unreliable, not pointing in the direction established by God through Christ. The confusion multiplies when the Church affirms those who have not followed the path of repentance and baptism that lead to a new life in Christ. Again, I remind you that it is not about identifying with the Church, but it is in finding our identity as a son of God. It is our new birth that makes us a son of God. The Word of God affirms our salvation that if we believe in our heart and confess with our mouth that Christ is Lord we will be saved. If the Church takes it upon itself to affirm people by any other standard they place in jeopardy the salvation of a soul.

> *"Woe to you, scribes and Pharisees, hypocrites,*
> *because you travel about on sea and land to*
> *make one proselyte; and when he becomes one,*
> *you make him twice as much a son of hell as*
> *yourselves."* (Mt 23:15 NAS)

The Church was given the message of salvation, deliverance from sin, and life everlasting. But if that message is compromised, then there is no redemption, and at best the Church provides false comfort for people on their way to hell. The Scribes and Pharisees were entrusted with the Word of God, but because of their compromises they produced sons of hell instead of sons of God. In essence, they taught people to become like they were instead of teaching the Law of God that molds people into the image of God. Today those who have been entrusted with the Word of God must share that word in its purity. When churches lose their identity as an assembly of the saints, the body of Christ, they are no longer the beacon of hope they were intended to be.

The loss of our national identity as a Christian nation is leaving a vast hole the world for those seeking hope and freedom. As churches across this nation are losing their identity as the body of Christ, the message of salvation is fading. If we, as individuals, lose our identity as Children of God, the world will be plunged into darkness. Those of us that remain must stand fast on the high ground! From here we can strengthen the churches. Together we can reestablish this nation that has lost its way. But it is only by holding to the high moral ground that there is hope.

CHAPTER 14
Politics and Healthcare

"And at that time many will fall away and will deliver up one another and hate one another. "And many false prophets will arise, and will mislead many. "And because lawlessness is increased, most people's love will grow cold. "But the one who endures to the end, he shall be saved." (Mt 24:10-13 NAS)

There is no doubt that the United States was established as a Christian nation. I briefly touched on the history of our nation that had its roots in the early settlements in the beginning of the 17th century. But there has been a great falling away from those Christian roots and the moral values they held. As we entered the 21st century the complete takeover of our educational system had been accomplished. God and His role in our national history had been cleansed from all but the vestiges of His once dominate role in providing wisdom and moral guidelines. It is now without that moral foundation that our population is easily led and manipulated by false prophets and false teachers. As those who remember God's historic role in our past crises, age and pass away, the voice of reason is being pushed to the side by a generation that does not know God.

With the rejection of God's central role in our identity as a people, our population is reverting to the paganism that stemmed from Man's fall in the Garden of Eden. Religion's role in a pagan culture becomes a means to control and manipulate the population. God is replaced with government. Government becomes the supplier of rights and blessings, or so people are deceived into believing. For all that government provides is first gleaned from the people. Is this not simply Man becoming God? Or is it a little deeper than that?

How is it possible to convince people that a government can take our rights and wealth from us and return it to us in a form that benefits us? The simple answer is that it can only do it through deception. Government is a very poor substitute for God. God has provided us with our abundant natural resources which provide everything we need for life. We can plant, till, and water but it is God who makes it grow and provides the blessings of rain in its season. Government is now insisting that we must allow it to control our resources so that it can control the weather and climate. God offers the blessing of good weather "if we live righteously". Government offers a stable climate if we submit to their control. Of course, government does not have the knowledge or ability to control the climate, but they do have their false prophets and false teachers.

It is the same in every area that the government promises to provide for us. Simple math will tell you that someone cannot take a dollar from you and then provide you with two dollars worth of services. But a government that borrows large sums of money can make you think they can. You or your children will eventually pay, with interest. Books could be written revealing the truth of how the wealth of America is being used to destroy what was once good about America and the freedom we once had. It has been estimated that it takes six dollars for the government to supply a poor person with one dollar's worth of food. Where is all the rest of the money going? It is supplying the fuel for the political agenda that promises to replace God.

Let me give you one more example of the false promises of government. Healthcare has become the number one issue at times. The false prophets claim that healthcare is a right. What does that mean? Who grants us that right? Government? Words have meaning, but as phrases become common rhetoric they take on new meaning.

Literally speaking, if healthcare is a right, then I have the right to take care of my health. If we compare healthcare to life (one of the unalienable rights proposed in our Declaration of Independence) we can put things into perspective. The right to life is a grant from God, only God can create life. Because it is a grant from God no man has the right to deprive us of that right. There are exceptions that are granted and explained in the Scripture, but they are based upon the judgment of God. We also need to note that the right to life comes with responsibility. The responsibility to maintaining that life falls first to the people who bring that life into the world (parents) and later to the individual. God has provided the natural resources and ability for us to provide the food, clothing, and shelter necessary for sustaining life, but it is our responsibility to maintain life. This is a very simplistic explanation, for the knowledge necessary for us to fulfill our responsibility has been passed down to us through the generations. We also have the Scriptures that give us the knowledge and wisdom necessary.

When people and politicians refer to "healthcare" as a right they have something entirely different in mind, even though they are using the language of our founding documents. The recognition of the rights referred to in our Declaration of Independence and Bill of Rights is on a different level than their assertion of "healthcare" as a right. This is just one example of the expansion of government and the role it plays in the life of the citizens of the country. Healthcare can only become a right granted by government to its citizens if government provides healthcare. Remember, government can only provide for its citizens something that it first took from them.

The beginning issue really is the provision of the cost of healthcare. We live in an age in which knowledge and technology have provided us with the ability to understand and treat injury and disease on many different levels. It is often complicated and sometimes very costly. This has become a blessing and a curse. All of this marvelous diagnostic equipment, medicine, and costly operations have caused the cost of healthcare to rise astronomically. Even the most basic of things like treating cuts and bruises has become expensive as we try to support this enormous machine we label "healthcare". So the issue politicians present as a government cure is for government to pay for your healthcare. But even if government had the money to pay for our healthcare it would not solve this problem. It is much more complicated than just money, and "healthcare" as a right gets to be "very" complicated.

First, government has to obtain the funds, and that means taxes. Then someone has to decide what treatments are going to be paid for and under which circumstances is each person eligible. Keep in mind that some treatments may cost hundreds of thousands of dollars, and there is no guarantee they will always work or how long they will extend a person's life. And it all gets much more complicated when we consider that the nature of healthcare is very individualistic. Do we dare ask why a person has their particular injury or disease? Do we address prevention? Is there a cure for stupidity or prevention for neglect? There actually is a cure for stupidity and prevention for neglect, but politics is not even part of the answer for these maladies.

What we find in our age of politics and its Orwellian language is that nothing is actually what it says it is. Healthcare should be considered a "right", we should be able to care for our health without the dictates of government. The responsibility for healthcare must rest with the individual, or in the case of children, with their parents. When advocates of government-controlled health care call healthcare a "right" they are talking about something entirely different. What they are actually calling for is making the treatment of health-related issues the responsibility of the government. For government to become responsible for our healthcare we must cede our "right" of healthcare to the government. Government then has the power to determine what and when we need care. Government must then extract the resources from the citizens to provide the services needed.

Many people have been persuaded that regardless of the cost, government healthcare can solve the problems and provide healthcare for all. But it simply does not work. One of the many reasons why it does not work is because those making important decisions about our health care are politicians and bureaucrats. Their main concerns are politics, money, power, and prestige, not necessarily in that order. Because their main concern is not your individual health they are easily influenced by corporate interests and political factions. Even if they become aware of the value of prevention and cause, they are unable to effectively address these most important aspects of healthcare. Because of the forces that drive politics, emphasis within healthcare is placed on a cure rather than a cause.

It is only when the responsibility for healthcare is left with the individual that prevention and cause can be adequately addressed. Only on the individual level can prevention be properly implemented. It is only dealing with people on the individual basis that caregivers can help identify potential causes. It is only in an atmosphere absent of politics that we can find and address the sometimes inconvenient truths that are uncovered through honest inquiry.

All of this brings us right back to the high moral ground. It is the ceding of the high moral ground that allows all the conversation about healthcare to go on without acknowledging that the root cause of most of our sickness is a departure from moral living. The best advice for prevention of sickness and disease is found in the Holy Scripture. The true cure for our ailments begins with our acknowledgement of sin. The best treatment for all our ailments begins with a meeting with the one and only Great Physician.

It is a fact that we cannot live forever in this world that has been affected by sin. But many of the ailments that people face have a direct cause from their sinful behavior. It is not politically correct to address our healthcare issues from the perspective of the high moral ground of God's Word. So people continue to suffer and die prematurely because we replace morality with politics.

CHAPTER 15
Global Warming

""Out of the south comes the storm, And out of the north the cold. "From the breath of God ice is made, And the expanse of the waters is frozen. "Also with moisture He loads the thick cloud; He disperses the cloud of His lightning. "And it changes direction, turning around by His guidance, That it may do whatever He commands it On the face of the inhabited earth. "Whether for correction, or for His world, Or for lovingkindness, He causes it to happen."
(Job 37:9-13 NAS)

Weather or Not

Weather is part of every news report, every day. In spite of the fact that we can in our modern society, remain indoors, the weather will affect our lives. For those who work outdoors, the effect is personal and can determine many of the directions and actions of their day. All of us are affected by weather, if not directly then indirectly, for it affects food production, construction, transportation and almost everything in one way or another. When we consider the occasional extreme weather, it can be much more dramatic. In minutes, it can alter the course of your life or end it.

Of course, those who are pushing the "global warming" agenda will tell you that it is not about the weather, but the change in climate; climatology versus meteorology. They say the reason for this is because it is hard to promote their agenda through fear, when the evidence of climate change is remote from where people live. Fear of global warming is hard to promote when people are experiencing severe cold from an arctic blast; however, when we are experiencing a record hot spell, then it is all about the weather and global warming.

Since the time of the flood, in Noah's day, mankind has been dealing with climate change. Books could be written on just the little we know about the effects climate change has had on mankind throughout history. Generally speaking, climate change usually happens gradually enough that people can adjust to the changes. Weather, on the other hand, can be dramatic. Even with our modern technology, it cannot be accurately predicted. In reality, climate and weather cannot be separated, for they are part of a very complex global system, marvelously designed to make the planet a habitable place for life. There is a great variety of climatic conditions that exist around the globe. Each of these climates has differing average weather patterns and differing extreme weather events. Geologic evidence reveals that in the past, climatic conditions may have been much different than we have today.

I am simply giving you this brief summary to show you how ridiculous the assertions of the global warming alarmists are. They claim that our present warming trend is due to human activity. They claim that in the future, human activity will dramatically alter the climate, adversely making the environment increasingly hostile. They claim that the major driver of the warming climate is the increase of CO2 in the atmosphere. The bottom line is that man-made climate change is going to destroy the planet.

The Agenda

According to climate alarmists, we have reached a tipping point with the accumulation of CO2 in the atmosphere. We must unite the entire population to combat this threat. Their claim is that if we do not act now, it will soon be too late and the planet is doomed. The questions we have to ask are: Why do they think that they are right? What if they are right? What is their proposed solution? What are the effects of their solution?

This whole issue of "global warming" is very complex, and would take a lot of time to fully explore. I believe that an in-depth study would reveal this issue as a hoax. That does not mean that there are not a multitude of people sincerely promoting this idea because they are genuinely concerned. As with any other issue, good intentions do not overrule the truth. What I am attempting here is to view this issue from the high moral ground. From this perspective, the facts look different than they do from a lower vantage point. If we just look at a few simple facts, we will realize that there are agendas driving this issue. It simply is not about the facts that can be verified.

So what do we know? CO2 levels are increasing over the last few years since we have been able to accurately measure them. CO2 is a greenhouse gas, and is essential for plant growth and life, in general, on this planet. Over the last 100 years, our overall global temperature has raised approximately 1.5 degrees. Temperature in the last 20 years has remained almost the same. Over this period, the sea levels continue to rise steadily every year. Population has grown, in my lifetime, from 2.5 billion to 6.5 billion. People contribute to the excess CO2 in our atmosphere in a multitude of ways.

The rise in temperature over the last 100 years has actually made most climates more hospitable, not less. What seems more amazing is that our increased population, and our burning of fossil fuels has not warmed our planet more than it has. So if life on earth is better than it was 100 years ago, what is the fear about? It is all based upon speculation about how the climate will change, and the effects it will have. These projections are mainly based upon computer models. In essence, these fears are based upon prophesies made by scientists, not actual facts. There are a lot of assumptions and conjecture involved in these computer models. Accurate measurements of atmospheric conditions are relatively new. Conditions from the past are based largely upon interpretation of evidence left behind. In addition to this, we know that none of the models presented so far have proven to be accurate in their predictions. In fact, all of their predictions have failed miserably.

There is no logical reason why we, as a country, should dramatically alter our way of life based simply upon the conjecture and climate models that have proven to be inaccurate. The promotion of this theory does fit well with the agendas of many different groups whose intent is to promote their own wealth and power. If we are willing to look at all of history, we will see that there have been attempts to create a one-world government since the time of the building of the city and tower of Babel. The behind-the-scenes agenda has always been Satan's attempt to unite the world under his direction, in opposition to God. Global warming provides a platform to bring nations together under the direction of one voice. Until now, God has always thwarted that agenda, and provided opportunity for choice through the division of nations.

The Other Agenda

Coming back to the high moral ground we have to view this issue from the revealed Word of God. God created this world and it is marvelously designed. Climate is much more complex than even our modern technology has observed. The very idea that mankind is going to be able to maintain control of the temperature of this planet, simply through curtailing the burning of fossil fuels, is absurd. Even simple math will render this concept to be ridiculous without removing most of the seven billion people. If God had not built marvelous intricacies into the model of this planet and its climate, we would have destroyed ourselves long ago. This planet was made as a home for people. God gave this planet to man to govern. It does well when we follow God's precepts.

It is the acknowledgement of God, and faith in His Word, that created the real division between God's faithful, and the prophets of "Global Warming". It is only logical that people, who have been convinced that the world and all we know is a series of random accidents, would be easily driven to fear by the slightest deviation in temperature. For those of us who believe the voice of the Creator, our faith is in God and His Word. Our attention needs to be on those things that really move the forces for good or evil. It is amazing that human activity has not affected the earth's temperature more than it has. This is because of God's marvelous design.

We could go in depth on this subject, and consider the many factors that are involved. We could delve into the historical knowledge that we do have, and shed much light on this subject; however, the conclusion would essentially be the same. God alone has the knowledge, wisdom and power to control the climate of this earth. Man's effect on the climate is contingent upon whether or not he is willing to live in harmony with God's eternal law.

We do know that in the past, climate and weather have been affected by human activity. The greatest disruption in climate is still affecting our planet. It was because of man's sin that God judged the earth and all that was in it, by the flood in Noah's day. We also know from God's Word that the climate, in Israel, has been altered at times because of the sins of His people. I do not know how much the weather and climates are going to be affected in our near future. I do know, from God's Word, that there are going to be distresses of many different kinds. I also know that it is not because we are burning fossil fuels, but because people are violating the moral laws of God.

There is a need to sound the warning, for judgment is coming. There are true prophets who prophesy from a proven model. There is a solution that provides for salvation. As Christians, we also have an agenda, and that is the salvation of souls. God may be willing to damage the planet to save souls. There are those who are willing to destroy souls to save the planet.

CHAPTER 16

A Moment of Silence

_____

"And it came about that while He was praying in a certain place, after He had finished, one of His disciples said to Him, "Lord, teach us to pray just as John also taught his disciples." And He said to them, "When you pray, say: 'Father, hallowed be Thy name. Thy kingdom come. 'Give us each day our daily bread. 'And forgive us our sins, For we ourselves also forgive everyone who is indebted to us. And lead us not into temptation.'"'" (Lu 11:1-4 NAS)

There is a feeling of exhilaration as we experience freedom and the ability to do as we please. The joy of this experience only finds fulfillment when what we wish to do is in the realm of our choosing. From the high moral ground we can experience this freedom without robbing someone else of their opportunity to also have freedom. Through our trust in God and His Word we learn to truly love and do good. Standing on this ground we can endure our life in this sin infested world while at the same time experiencing a freedom from the bondage it seeks to impose on us. We are citizens of an eternal kingdom even while we are dwelling in a world dominated by the influence of Satan. Prayer is our connection and the avenue of our essential communication with that eternal kingdom.

As an individual citizen in this eternal kingdom we recognize that each of us has purpose and meaning in our limited existence on Earth. Foremost, we are ambassadors of the love that emulates from that kingdom. Freed from the bondage of sin and death we are only bound by the Law of Love, and with joy we submit to its dictates. But our freedom is a freedom of spirit, and while we live on earth we are often physically bound by the dictates of evil men and the forces of nature in a broken world. As individuals against great odds our purpose would seem hopeless if it were not for our ability to connect with our heavenly kingdom that is not bound and knows no bounds. Is it any wonder that the forces of this world would try to restrict our prayers? Is it any wonder that they would try to intimidate us into limiting our prayers according to their dictates?

God created this world as a dwelling place for mankind. God gave Man dominion over all the Earth and everything herein. In Man's arrogance people have often abused and misused this Earth and its resources. Mankind has attempted to build a kingdom of our own without regard for our Creator and Benefactor. In so doing, people are continually violating the Law of the Universe, the Law of God, which is Love.

But occasionally people are pulled up short and reminded that life is a gift, and that gift can vanish in a moment. Often we are confronted with the effects of unbridled lust and the death and destruction it brings. Often we are confronted with the forces of nature that render us helpless under its relentless power. Storms, earthquakes, and volcanoes often bring the hardest of souls to their knees. Standing before the lifeless bodies of those we cared for reminds us of our vulnerabilities and the reality of death.

All of our knowledge, all of our technology, all of the king's horses and all the king's men cannot put humpty dumpty back together again. It is at these times that our human heart cries out for something bigger and greater than Man that would bring us comfort and hope. We cry out for meaning beyond the lifeless corpse in front of us. We cry out for hope, desiring something beyond the grave that will give us meaning and an end to suffering. It is in these times that even the ungodly pray, seeking comfort, seeking hope.

> *"For while I was passing through and examining the objects of your worship, I also found an altar with this inscription, 'TO AN UNKNOWN GOD.' What therefore you worship in ignorance, this I proclaim to you."* (Ac 17:23 NAS)

Only God has the power and authority to call back a person into this earthly realm. On occasion He has done this to reveal to us who He is. But the message is to the living for it has been appointed for man to die and then the judgment. There is only one God, the Creator of all that is. But most people do not know Him. That does not mean that there are not a multitude of religions and false gods. Satan exists and there are demons, but they are not gods. Satan continues to entice people to play god in the world they live in, but that does not make them God. And then there are the gods that are the creation of people's hands or their imagination, but they are not God.

Remember the definition of the Moral High Ground: right standing before God. If we are on this ground then we know God and recognize Him only as God. And yet I have heard those who claim the title of Christian to stand in a crowd and call for a moment of silence. I find this reprehensible. I understand that many have done this in ignorance and that is why I am striving to write this book. When we as people come to a junction in our lives when we acknowledge that we as people are helpless, we need to look to God. There was a time in this Christian nation that most people knew what that meant. But in our present politically correct culture most people do not. They have been taught that equal respect should be shown to everyone's concept of god. A moment of silence is a call for everyone to reach out to their own god for hope and comfort. How can a Christian do that in good conscience?

We cannot cede the high ground. Coming down to their level brings no real hope or comfort. If we are to say anything, and we should, we should point people to their Creator and offer a prayer to the God of heaven. We can as Christians intercede for these people in their ignorance and pray for the grace of God to be present. We can as Christian cry for mercy and speak with the authority of our Lord and Savior, Jesus Christ. These times of crisis are an opportunity to show our love for our fellow human beings and share with them the hope that God has given through Jesus Christ.

What we should NOT do is call for a moment of silence and show equal respect for the gods of man's hand and their imagination, and the only true God who truly cares for them. Why would we pander to their politically correct culture? After all, politics do not exist in the kingdom of God. Why would we cede the high ground? On their level comfort is meaningless, for there is no hope in death without Jesus Christ. If you have truly come to know God through Jesus Christ, then stand your ground.

We need to take any opportunity afforded to us to point people to the only source of hope and comfort. Rather than asking for a moment of silence, we should request that we be allowed to call on our Lord and Savior, Jesus Christ, to graciously minister to those who are suffering. By simply requesting; "May I pray?" we may have opportunity to share the love of God. We have a standing before our heavenly Father that they do not have. Who knows what effect our expressions of faith will have at these crucial times in our lives? As Christians we know that what people need most during times of crisis, is Jesus. He is the only true source of hope and comfort.

CHAPTER 17
Offenses

"Woe unto the world because of offences! for it must needs be that offences come; but woe to that man by whom the offence cometh!"
(Mt 18:7 AV)

U nderstanding offenses is very important. As with every other subject it is important that we view offences from God's perspective. Every one of us has experienced being on both ends of an offense. We can offend and we can be offended. There are offenses against people and there are offenses against God. There are those who are easily offended and then there are those who are not easily offended. Some are wounded by an offense, and some take an offense as a reason for wounding another. Some are focused on offenses against themselves. Others readily pick up the offenses of others.

"But whoso shall offend one of these little ones which believe in me, it were better for him that a millstone were hanged about his neck, and that he were drowned in the depth of the sea."
(Mt 18:6 AV)

There is no better place to start in our discussion of offenses than to consider the effect we have on children. God is pretty protective of His little ones and has a serious warning for those who offend even one of these little ones. Obviously, God does not want any harm to come to His little children. The word "offend" in this text literally means to cause to stumble or sin.

"But Jesus said, "Let the children alone, and do not hinder them from coming to Me; for the kingdom of heaven belongs to such as these."
(Mt 19:14 NAS)

Children, especially little children, are most vulnerable to the effects of our speech and actions. They are learning about the world around them and developing their own character. It is obvious that this is the most important area in which we are to be concerned about offenses. This is where we need to be most careful to guard our speech and actions from offending. An offense at a tender young age can cause one of these little ones to be propelled on a destructive path that may be the cause of much pain for many people and end in eternal destruction.

I recall hearing a man tell of his experience as a young child. Coming from a family that did not attend church he had begun to attend a Sunday school through the invitation of a neighbor. He enjoyed Sunday school and the stories and songs he was learning. On one occasion his Sunday school teacher featured him and some of his friends on the platform for the whole con-gregation, singing some songs they had learned. It so happened that afterwards he overheard a couple of ladies discussing how inappropriately this young boy was dressed for being on the platform. He was humiliated and said he never darkened the door of a church again for the next twenty-five years.

Today dress codes are not as vogue in churches as they were in times past, but this story illustrates how little comments can have huge impacts on those that are young, sensitive, and vulnerable. These young lives are in the process of being molded into a good or bad character. They are very impressionable, which makes it important that we not only avoid bad impressions, but we are careful to inject good impressions. If we take to heart the seriousness of offending one of these little ones from Jesus' warning, then we will avoid those caustic comments and actions that can have such devastating effects on these young lives. But, I think we also need to acknowledge that it is possible that we can inadvertently negatively affect these young lives without knowing it. It often seems like it is impossible to avoid misunderstandings that may cause a negative effect. I think the answer to this can be seen in the example Jesus gave for us. He encouraged that the children would come to Him. It is the positive input into these young lives that is most likely to clear up any misunderstandings they may have and avoid serious offenses.

Living in the Now

"If therefore you are presenting your offering at the altar, and there remember that your brother has something against you, leave your offering there before the altar, and go your way; first be reconciled to your brother, and then come and present your offering." (Mt 5:23-24 NAS)

"Never pay back evil for evil to anyone. Respect what is right in the sight of all men. If possible,

> *so far as it depends on you, be at peace with all men."* (Ro 12:17-18 NAS)

> *"Pursue peace with all men, and the sanctification without which no one will see the Lord."* (Heb 12:14 NAS)

Offenses are not necessarily more serious as we grow older, but often people take them more seriously than they did as children. I have known people who have carried grudges for years or decades. Historically, there have been feuds that lasted for generations. But, as Christians we are instructed to handle offenses quickly and not let them fester. It does not matter if we were offended or if we were the offender, our instruction is to do everything in our power to settle the matter and be at peace with those we encounter. Sometimes there is a cost we have to pay, sometimes because of our offense and sometimes because of someone else's sin. It may not seem fair that we pay the price for another's offense, but it is often in the interest of the Kingdom of God that we do so. Remember this is what Christ did for us.

> *"Then Peter came and said to Him, "Lord, how often shall my brother sin against me and I forgive him? Up to seven times?" Jesus *said to him, "I do not say to you, up to seven times, but up to seventy times seven."* (Mt 18:21-22 NAS)

For those of us who have experienced the love of God, we are continually being amazed at the depth and breadth of the love of God. We are gaining an understanding of the words and love of Jesus that the world simply does not understand. We who have embraced His love are also learning to show that love to those who do not understand love. By the example of our Lord we have learned of this love, and by our example the world can glimpse what true love really is. Without love the instructions of our Lord seem unrealistic and unfair. It is the love of God that dwells within us that makes us willing and able to forgive those who offend us.

> *"Above all, keep fervent in your love for one another, because love covers a multitude of sins."* (1Pe 4:8 NAS)

As a Christian, an ambassador of Christ, we can and should endure offenses, and love in return, as our Lord has by example shown us. These verses from I Peter at first seem unfair, ignoring justice. We know that God is a God of justice, and He has revealed that in the end justice will be served. But through an understanding of love and mercy we can see how, that through love, mercy can triumph over justice (James 2:13). It is only with this under-standing that we can find acceptance of the following verses.

> *"For this finds favor, if for the sake of conscience toward God a man bears up under sorrows when suffering unjustly. For what credit is there if, when you sin and are harshly treated, you endure it with patience? But if when you do what is right and suffer for it you patiently endure it, this finds favor with God. For you have been called for this purpose, since Christ also suffered for you, leaving you an example for you to follow in His steps,"* (1Pe 2:19-21 NAS)

Let me summarize: do what is right, suffer for doing what is right, and then endure the suffering patiently. Let's cap all that off with the statement that we have been called for this purpose. Why would we accept this calling that is so unfair? We should accept it for the same reason Christ did. It is all about love and the salvation of souls, that without the love of God, will face the judgment of God. Our suffering is for the purpose of giving people an example of the love of God, that they would understand that through His suffering, and sometimes ours, mercy can triumph over justice. Through repentance they can also become recipients of the grace of God for salvation.

The bottom line is that we as Christians cannot be easily offended, but are willing to suffer offense for the sake of others. A volume could be written on this subject that is rooted in the love of God that has come to us through Christ Jesus and His sacrificial death on the cross for us. This love that is birthed also in us is the source of our love for our brethren. It is also the source of our love for those around us, and our desire to share with them the love of God that provides salvation for all who will receive it. I leave you with this brief instruction of how we as Christians should deal with offenses that can be categorized as sin, and move on to balance this with the world's perception of offenses.

Viewing Offenses From the High Ground

"So then let us pursue the things which make for peace and the building up of one another. Do not tear down the work of God for the sake of food. All things indeed are clean, but they are evil for the man who eats and gives offense. It

is good not to eat meat or to drink wine, or to do anything by which your brother stumbles." (Ro 14:19-21 NAS)

From a Biblical perspective, that which is offensive is either sinning or an action that causes someone to stumble in their faith. Sin is an offense to God for it violates the Law of Love. The violation of God's Law is injurious and destructive to the creation of God of which we were intended to be the crowning glory. As we mature, our vision expands and we can see more clearly the effects of sin. But God's view is inclusive of all that is and all that will be. Our faith is based upon this fact that God knows all, and if He forbids us to do something it is because it is not good for us, for it violates the Law of Love. God has revealed His law through His Word, exposing sin and evil and the inevitable judgment for sin. As we mature as believers following the example of our Lord we will not be easily offended, for our aim and goal will be the salvation of souls, trusting God that our salvation is secure. That is why we will be able to bear the offensive nature of the unredeemed, as Christ so graciously modeled for us.

The subject of offenses in Scripture is often focused on the young and the immature. Jesus used children to emphasize the care we need to exercise on their behalf. Here that principle is being applied to those who are young in the faith, those who may have weak faith. Whether we are talking about the physical or the spiritual, youth and immaturity does not have the knowledge to always discern between good and bad. We often have guidelines for children so that they avoid situations they may face for which they are not prepared for. If we look at the history of any church organization we will see guidelines that are not directly from the Scripture. If we truly understand the principles of God as revealed in Scripture we may find fault with some of these guidelines. We may feel that they impose restrictions on our behavior that God never intended. But what the Scripture is trying to teach us here in Romans is that our focus needs to first consider those of tender young faith. As mature members of the family of faith it is our foremost duty to protect the young. If that restricts our freedom, then so be it. If my behavior could possibly cause someone to stumble in their faith, then I better not do it.

Offenses do come about through the violation of God's commands. But even if we are not in violation of a literal command of God, we can be violating the Law of Love if our actions cause someone weak in faith to stumble.

> *"For through your knowledge he who is weak is ruined, the brother for whose sake Christ died. And thus, by sinning against the brethren and wounding their conscience when it is weak, you sin against Christ. Therefore, if food causes my brother to stumble, I will never eat meat again, that I might not cause my brother to stumble."*
> (1Co 8:11-13 NAS)

Ceding the High Ground on Offenses

> *"And after He called the multitude to Him, He said to them, "Hear, and understand. "Not what enters into the mouth defiles the man, but what proceeds out of the mouth, this defiles*

**the man." Then the disciples *came and *said
to Him, "Do You know that the Pharisees were
offended when they heard this statement?"**
(Mt 15:10-12 NAS)

If we take the subject of offenses to the low ground we will stir
up a hornets' nest. Historically, offenses have been the cause
of much discontent and grief. Offenses have been the cause of
hatred that has resulted in feuds, duels, and wars. As residents
of the High Ground, we are to be above this and understand
the root of many of these offenses is the bondage to sin and
its affects. Love enables us to tolerate offense directed toward
us. Love also compels us to avoid becoming an offense. But we
must hold to the high ground or love will be consumed by hate.

Remember that offenses from a Biblical perspective are either
sin or the cause of someone stumbling and falling from grace.
Conversely, the world's concept of an offense is something that
violated their personal desire. Their desire is usually that they
feel good about themselves and that everyone would agree
with them. In a previous section I identified this in the search
for identity and affirmation. Both of these can only be satisfied
in our reconciliation with God. But without God this desire is
fueled to produce pride and arrogance that often is offended,
resulting in hatred to avoid depression.

From the high ground of God's Word we can understand what
really is offensive, but from the world's perspective an offense
has a completely different definition. If we allow ourselves to
be drawn down to their perspective concerning offenses, the
gospel will be turned on its head. As a Christian we are to strive

to not be offensive to others. From the high ground that means that we do not sin against others or cause them to stumble or sin. But from the world's perspective being offensive is violating someone's personal comfort. As a light in a dark place, that makes us and our message of the Gospel offensive. Jesus' words were offensive to the Pharisees because they revealed truth that they did not want to hear. When we share the Words of God in a sinful world it is going to offend them, whether they accept it as truth or not. But from God's perspective we are not being offensive, but rather we are sharing the Love of God.

Again, I direct our attention to Jesus. Jesus never allowed the opinions of others to alter His words or His mission, and neither should we. The revelation of God reveals sin in a sinful world. It is sin that is the offense, not the exposure of it. We need to keep our eyes focused on Jesus as our example, and keep our feet planted in the high moral ground of His Word. If we do not we will be intimidated by the voices of this world that would attempt to silence the message that has come down from heaven. Jesus preached righteousness and lived righteousness, and we should do the same. Jesus' message is one of redemption, reconciling man to God. That reconciliation comes through acknowledgment of sin, repentance, and cleansing from all unrighteousness, and that is offensive to those who revel in their sin and pride.

As you can see, our instructions about offenses from the Scripture are totally turned upside down if we substitute the world's concept of offense with God's definition of offense. We need to be very careful lest we cede the high ground and allow the world's perspectives to affect our speech and actions which are dictated by the high moral values revealed in God's Word.

> *"Then Jesus answering said unto them, Go your way, and tell John what things ye have seen and heard; how that the blind see, the lame walk, the lepers are cleansed, the deaf hear, the dead are raised, to the poor the gospel is preached. And blessed is he, whosoever shall not be offended in me."* (Lu 7:22-23 AV)

> *"When Jesus knew in himself that his disciples murmured at it, he said unto them, Doth this offend you?"* (Joh 6:61 AV)

Happy is the man who is not offended by our Lord Jesus Christ. From the world's perspective Jesus and His message are offensive. Jesus did not conform to the expectations of the religious world, and it offended them. The righteousness of God that came to us in human form was offensive to standards of men. Jesus came with a message of mercy, grace, and love, and yet people were offended. Why were they offended? They were offended because their sin was exposed and the reception of God's love was contingent upon their repentance. Jesus brought love on a higher level. Pride and short-sightedness cause people to seek comfort in their sin. Jesus' love came to rescue people from sin and set them free from the bondage to it. Happy is the person who does not find this offensive.

The question is: does Jesus offend you? From the world's perspective God's judgments are offensive. But, if we view Jesus from the high ground we see that all He is and all He does stems from the Love of God that has come down to us. There is nothing offensive about that. This is the message from heaven that we are to share with the world. If we allow the offenses of men to compromise the message of the Gospel, then the Love of God will be to no effect. In essence, we will be merely comforting people on their way to hell, rather than pointing them to Jesus who can save them from sin and death and provide eternal life.

CHAPTER 18
Faith, Hope, and Love

---

*"But now abide faith, hope, love, these three; but
the greatest of these is love."* (1Co 13:13 NAS)

W e have preserved for us in the Bible a record of God's
revelation to mankind. Its accuracy can be attributed
to the faithfulness of God and the diligence of His servants.
We have every reason in the world to trust this record as being
truth. God's Word has been confirmed by His Son and His Spirit.
Those who have lived by this Word also testify of its truth. The
Word was given to us that we might have Life.

The Scripture has given us a lens through which we can view
the world. Without this lens all that we see is cloudy and dark.
Those who choose to ignore the revelation of God are as blind
men groping in the dark. The world they see exists only in their
imaginations. In their mind the world is a place that was created
through evil, death, and suffering. Out of chaos and random
confusion mankind has arisen to finally take hold of his destiny.
They believe that through using emerging technology mankind
is now on the verge of leveraging his knowledge to eventually
establishing an eternal existence for himself and his posterity.
Man has now come to the place where he believes nothing is
impossible for him as he is becoming like god.

You may think that no one really believes what I have just described. But yet, in many ways people's actions seem to reflect that this is what they do believe. In spite of the fact that we are faced with reality checks on a daily basis, people still try to live in a fantasy world of their own making. Increasingly, people are being encouraged to live in a fantasy world. Never in all of history has the push been so strong, with a multitude of voices and a multitude of choices. But the laws of the universe remain unchanged. Truth remains.

Those who still choose to view everything through the lens of Scripture know the truth, and the truth has set them free. It is as if scales have fallen from their eyes and they can see. These people are the light of the world. Without the light that shines from heaven there is no hope for this world that is perishing. No amount of wishing will change that. That is why the testimony of those who can see is so important in the world, and why the enemy is so intent on trying to deceive us into thinking that we can gain by giving up our standing on the high moral ground of God's Truth.

As I conclude this discussion intended to encourage people to stand fast on the high ground without ceding one inch, I will emphasize these three pillars, faith, hope, and love. This is just a reminder, for I have touched on these all before. Bear with me as I go over them one more time. These three simple words can be turned on their head if their definitions are tampered with. As with many words in the English dictionary, their meaning can change with time. We have to define them within the text that we find them. I am talking about Biblical Faith, Biblical Hope, and Biblical Love.

Faith

Faith in our culture has come to mean a lot of things. But in the Bible it is speaking about confidence in God and His Word, which are one and the same. Faith is about believing in something that we cannot see. We believe it because God has told us it is true. We have faith in what He has said because His record is perfect. From this revelation we see that all God declares beforehand comes to pass just as He has declared. So our faith is not a blind faith that has no foundation, but it is established on God who is faithful.

The word faith has been compromised by using it to refer to religions of the world. Faith in God has no comparison; it stands alone on an unshakable foundation of truth. Only the Bible has stood the test of time, accurately revealing the truth. Biblical faith is an unwavering confidence in God and His Word. This is not a blind faith, but rather confidence in established truth. Earlier I discussed how new discoveries in science are continuing to verify the Words of God spoken long ago. Those that have placed their faith in God are always rewarded. Noah's faith placed him on the right side of the door of the ark. Faith in God is about trusting Him for things we cannot see, but if God said it, believe it or not, it is real.

Hope

Hope in our modern language offers little conciliation. Its usual usage reflects mere wishful thinking or a desire to want something to happen or be true. Often hope does rise to a higher level when the expression of our desire has expectations of fulfillment. We have all experienced joy as our hope was fulfilled and disappointment when it was not.

But there is an archaic definition of hope defined as: trust, reliance. This is the hope referred to in Scripture. This is hope that is founded on our faith in God and His promises. Biblical hope is anticipation of the fulfillment of the promises of God, looking forward with assurance for the fulfillment of our greatest desire. The more we learn about our Savior, the bigger our picture is of what this all entails. Simply put, we anticipate Christ's return because it ushers in the beginning of the fulfillment of our desire that where He is, we will be too.

Even here, in a discussion that is usually among believers, it is possible to cede the high ground and direct people's focus on things that are temporal, such as avoiding suffering or tribulation. Hope is that which is based upon the Word of God so that those who hope will never be disappointed. For we have this word from God that the fulfillment of our hope will exceed all that we think or imagine.

Love

I wrote earlier about the four different Greek words that in our English translations are translated as love. Our modern language has confused the matter even more. Our modern, secular culture has debased love even further, bringing it down to an animalistic nature. So we need to be careful to clarify that the love we are speaking about here is "agape" love. This is God's love toward us. This love is not based upon feelings or circumstances, for it is the unwavering choice of the giver. This love is best described as caring for and desiring the best for its recipient. This love is expressed using all the means at one's disposal to provide the best of conditions for the one that is loved.

We who are recipients of God's love are to learn from Him how to express this love toward those we are called to love. We have to admit that our love is limited by the resources at our disposal. The greatest love we can give stems from the gifts that we have received from heaven. Those gifts begin with our knowledge of the love of God, and that is where our loving begins to those whom we love. But think about it. Think about the resources at God,s disposal. Think about how He offered His only begotten Son to die for us. He has withheld nothing from us if we will accept His Love. Now that is what I call Love.

"But now abide faith, hope, love, these three; but the greatest of these is love." (1Co 13:13 NAS)

Standing Firm

"Therefore, take up the full armor of God, that you may be able to resist in the evil day, and having done everything, to stand firm." (Eph 6:13 NAS)

Having the faith, hope and love that come from God above, we stand on the high moral ground. We cannot cede one inch of that holy ground without jeopardizing souls. God's message of truth must remain pure or truth will be compromised. Our faith needs to be unwavering if we are to avoid unnecessary suffering. If we stand firm our hope will be fulfilled. God has provided all that we need to stand. It is therefore up to us to stand. Love conquers all.

Epilogue

"As for me, I heard but could not understand; so I said, "My lord, what will be the outcome of these events?" And he said, "Go your way, Daniel, for these words are concealed and sealed up until the end time. "Many will be purged, purified and refined; but the wicked will act wickedly, and none of the wicked will understand, but those who have insight will understand." (Da 12:8-10 NAS)

The lessons of history can easily be lost in one generation. History confirms that this is true and we are witnessing it happening in our generation. Our society here in North America is in the process of self-destructing. As I write this, the "Rule of Law" is being trumped by hate and discontent. Those who wish to overthrow our government and its Godly foundation have clearly revealed their intentions. The various factions of evil have allied themselves in an attempt to overrule the checks and balances that once guarded our rights and freedoms. If they succeed, the whole world will suffer. These people are willing to turn over control of our nation to be ruled by those who follow the dictates of the evil one. Whether they understand what they are doing or not becomes irrelevant if the world falls under control of the council of the evil one.

God's children are the only thing standing in the gap. The intercession of God's people is what is standing between God and the destruction of this world. What will be the end of our present struggle? Honestly, I don't know. The world has survived many crises in the past and God is able to avert this one too. But I do know that there is coming a time when God will decide to clean everything up. For those who have chosen to follow Christ, that will be the day of our redemption. But for most people it will be a day of judgment.

> *"And they overcame him because of the blood of the Lamb and because of the word of their testimony, and they did not love their life even to death."* (Re 12:11 NAS)

If we do not cede the high ground we will overcome. We stand on this ground because Christ died for us. We stand as witnesses of the grace and power of God's love. Our stance and testimony is a plea for those around us to trust God and the power of His Word. Our love compels us to plead with them so that they can avoid the judgment of God that will condemn all evil, wiping it from the face of the earth. We cannot cede one inch of this high moral ground that reconciles us to God and allows us to live in harmony with Him for all of eternity. Our fate and that of those around us is counting on us to stand firm.

> *"And those who have insight will shine brightly like the brightness of the expanse of heaven, and those who lead the many to righteousness, like the stars forever and ever."* (Da 12:3 NAS)

CPSIA information can be obtained
at www.ICGtesting.com
Printed in the USA
FSHW011839100320
68000FS